THEY WA

THEY WALKED ON WATER

The Untold Story of
Wembley 1968

David Hinchliffe

Scratching Shed Publishing Ltd

Dedication

To all the players supported by Try Assist -
the Rugby League Benevolent Fund'

Contents

Foreword

By Mike 'Stevo' Stephenson

I'd just started to make in-roads into the Dewsbury first team and had played against both 1968 Challenge Cup finalists. It was always a dream - after playing for your country - to run out at Wembley, which I never got to do, but I haven't missed a final since, apart from when I went to play in Australia.

There were a group of lads I grew up with in Dewsbury and we used to save up so much a week to make the annual pilgrimage to the Twin Towers.

It was a big thing. You'd go down to London on the Friday and get on the drink, get ripped off by some restaurant and be appalled at the amount of money you'd have to pay for a flat beer, but it was all part of the tradition. We couldn't believe how much the hotels cost for a nine-foot square room, yet it all added to it.

We used to arrive at the stadium early because we loved the thought of strolling down Wembley Way, with all the mingling, crowd and atmosphere. That's the one thing I'm glad they retained with the new stadium, because that walk is just as important as the match.

In 1968, as we started our wander, it started to throw it down. I've never seen anything like it. Everyone was just soaked to the skin and we thought the game would be off. To make it worse, the Royal International Horse Show, I think it was, had been staged there the week before and the ground had been churned up.

Yet because this match was going to be on television, the ground staff , I believe, applied some green crystals to the surface. That made the pitch look great, but it caused the water to sit on the top.

I vividly recall seeing the players on their long walk out from behind the sticks - another great tradition - and, as they did, pools of water began to splash up. I remember thinking, 'This is going to be a nightmare for them.' We could not believe it.

Our gang were keen to see our friend from Dewsbury, Bernard Watson, playing for Leeds. It was his mistake, when the ball squirted under his boot, that led to the dramatic last try. We really felt for him... it was incredible.

Early on we'd seen winger John Atkinson desperately slide into the hoardings when chasing a ball - as he had to do to stop it going dead or, in those days, concede a contested scrum. Under normal conditions it would have just sat up nicely for him.

The tension throughout was amazing. It was like watching cartoons, we were just laughing.

Every time there was a tackle, the players disappeared under a plume of water. Leeds and Wakefield were the two best teams around at the time, so it should have been a real showpiece. There was no skill factor that day, it was about sheer guts and determination.

Don Fox was outstanding, man of the match by a country mile, but those dying seconds defined him.

When you know someone out there you feel it more and I'd played against Bernard all my junior career. He was a terrific player and I could see him dejected with his head in his hands as Don lined up the final kick; he was in torment because he thought his mistake had cost Leeds the cup.

Of course what happened after that was slow motion. I can still feel it now.

There was a split-second's gap of silence in the stadium after Don's kick went wide as everybody took in what had happened. Then the Leeds players erupted. On top of everything else, it cemented this game as the most memorable in the sport's history, even forty-five years on.

Its impact has been compounded by what happened afterwards to Don. I don't think he ever really got over it; a burden he had to carry through the rest of his life. Wherever he went he would be reminded and teased about it.

The following week Don was filmed kicking goals in his slippers, which perpetuated the myth even more. And to think he'd been the best player out there - winner of the Lance Todd Trophy. It weighed heavily upon him.

Everybody in the national stadium that day felt sad at the climax. There was hardly any jubilation, even from the Leeds fans. Walking back down Wembley Way, it was as though we were leaving a funeral.

Mike Stephenson
April 2013

Chapter One

The 'Watersplash' watershed

It was on the train returning from the Millennium Magic Super League weekend in Wales in 2011 when I realised that a decades-old wound had re-opened once more. The carriage was packed with travellers, the majority Leeds Rhinos supporters coming away from the national stadium in Cardiff after seeing their side defeat Bradford thanks to the awarding of a controversial penalty try. The previous time we'd been down there, for the inaugural round of games played under the same roof, Leeds had also beaten the Bulls in the final moments in similarly disputed circumstances.

'Just like 1968,' I said to a female Leeds supporter who appeared to be of a similar vintage to myself. 'Pardon,' she replied, quizzically. 'Just like the 1968 Cup final,' I repeated and, noting her totally blank expression added, 'You won that one because Wakefield were robbed by the awarding of a penalty try.'

The lady in question was clearly unknowing as to the particular circumstances of Wembley that fateful year and others in the carriage appeared similarly baffled. The group of family and friends I was with looked on despairingly and I noticed that my son was rolling his eyes. They had heard it all before and found it rather sad that this (almost) senior citizen could not pass a blue and amber scarf without launching into a 1968 tirade.

It was the never-to-be-forgotten year of protest, one that cultural historians have pointed out as crystallising the 'sixties revolution', when teenagers and students came of age as a voice in society. Yet here was I, of such an age at the time, by then politically active and excited by those voices calling for radical change, referring again to the lingering issue of a penalty try.

But it wasn't just the fact that my team lost that final and the chance to achieve the Challenge Cup and Championship double for the first time in their history. It was the manner in which we lost which has never gone away and, in particular, the fact that the continued retelling of the story of what happened that day is unfailingly incomplete.

It was, we are told, all about a last second missed conversion in front of the posts. But then, it wasn't just any failed attempt. It was - and still is - the single most iconic image of rugby league, even if the oft-played footage is black and white and grainy.

Even those with limited knowledge of or interest in our sport are aware of what happened at the end of that game. So much of history is slimmed down to simplifications but the perceived wisdom of this encounter is that it was all down to a slice off a boot, an error that caused Eddie Waring to utter the immortal words, 'ee's a poor lad.' For me, that was always a gross misrepresentation of a remarkable game which was played in the most appalling conditions and contained a great deal more equally worthy of note.

A deeply-held, life-long grievance is probably not the best motivation for writing a book. But, if I'm honest, it has been a significant factor in driving my research into the 1968 Rugby League Challenge Cup final. It was only my second ever visit to the capital; my first ever visit to the Twin Towers, supporting my team, Wakefield Trinity and I came away with a sense of injustice, shared with thousands of other Belle Vue supporters, which has remained with me ever since. And that iniquity has been reinforced and repeated over decades by the retelling of a fundamentally partial history of this match.

I have had the great good fortune to lead a full and interesting life which has enabled me to see the world and meet some quite remarkable people. So, on the face of it, letting this sense of injustice simmer for more than four decades might seem strange. But that 1968 final - although we were not to know it at the time - was to very much mark the end of the great era of Wakefield Trinity which I and many others had the privilege to grow up in.

For some of the Wakefield folk of my generation that turbulent May day all those years ago marked, perhaps, the end of the sixties' adolescent dream, which makes it even harder to forgive and forget. What became known as the 'Watersplash' can be seen for some of us as a watershed, one we have been reminded of time and again ever since.

But there were other reasons for wanting to investigate this historic occasion. It was not just any final. It was, arguably, rugby league's most famous final. It was certainly the sport's most controversial. Played on a pitch flooded by torrential rain, the fact that the game was given the go-ahead was in itself highly contentious. The players clearly had difficulties remaining upright, mistake-free handling was impossible and the kicking was a lottery.

The award of a penalty try by the referee in the midst

of all that is a decision still hotly debated by followers of the game and the television recording of the last moments, enshrined by commentary which has passed into folklore, in the same way as Kenneth Wolstenholme's 'They think it's all over...', is surely the most famous in the long and distinguished history of the thirteen-man game.

In sporting - and, indeed, non-sporting company - I have argued my corner on the outcome of this match many thousand times. My personal views are already on the record so it would be nonsense to pretend genuine objectivity in my treatment of the subject. I clearly don't occupy the neutral corner in this particular contest but, in writing my account, have endeavoured to ensure that this important story fully reflects the sometimes markedly different perspectives of the opposing camps.

And, while I write these musings as a lifelong supporter of the red, white and blue, more importantly, I also approach the subject as a very proud follower of a sport which has been such an important part of my life; one whose history, traditions, values and struggles I hold very dear and which are, essentially still, a metaphor for the 'real' world.

If I set out to right a wrong it is probably up to others to determine whether I have succeeded. But I hope I have now established, once and for all, the fact that the 1968 Rugby League Challenge Cup final was about a good deal more than a missed conversion. This full story is long overdue.

Chapter Two

The Merrie City in the sixties and the icing on the cake

It was almost forty-four years on from the dramas and trauma of Wembley 1968 and Halloween. On a dark and dismal autumn evening I am seated in the pleasant front room of David and Delia Hebblethwaite's house on the outskirts of York watching, on their large, wall-mounted, television screen, a DVD of the black and white BBC coverage of that match. David's particular interest in the final is that his father, John Pearson Hebblethwaite, was the referee that day; the culmination of a long and distinguished career with the whistle and the proudest moment of his life.

I was particularly struck that night that David Hebblethwaite and I - both in our late teens at the time - approach the recollection of this match from markedly differing perspectives. For me, a sense of bitterness over a hugely controversial decision by his dad that fateful afternoon has stayed with me ever since. For him it remains a matter of immense satisfaction seeing his father centre stage in this most memorable of matches, played in front of millions and still vividly remembered by so many. But it must also have been a sad reminder of the fact that, within less than a year of that occasion, both his parents had died in the most tragic of circumstances.

Against this background it seems almost crass to try and expand on why the '68 final was so very significant for me. Indeed, bearing in mind his own experiences of the time - like me, still in his formative years - it is hard not to feel some guilt over having carried the emotional baggage for so long. But it wasn't just that it was a truly remarkable match that no-one who was present would ever forget it whatever the reason. Or that, for those of a Wakefield persuasion, the perceived unfairness remains unresolved. It's particular and very special resonance for me was where it fitted into my life and, specifically, my growing up. It constituted an amazing finale to a period that left me with some wonderful memories.

In 1968, I was coming towards the end of my teens. In some respects, I genuinely regretted the fact, because to have been a teenager in that decade was an amazing privilege. I recall it as a period of relative prosperity and great optimism. And for someone with an interest in rock music it was an incredible era to have lived through, witnessing the crude rock and roll of the late fifties transform into the wonderful, wide-ranging genres that made up the music of the 'swinging sixties'.

Wakefield may not have been Liverpool - or the west coast of the States for that matter - but in the ABC Regal, down Kirkgate, we had a cinema that staged numerous touring one-nighters featuring many of the top names of the era. It was the Merrie City's very own Cavern Club. If we didn't have tickets for a show, or had seen the first house of the evening, my mates and I would hang around the stage door at the back listening to the music from outside and waiting to get autographs.

I still cherish - as a kid of thirteen or fourteen - walking from the Regal to the old Strafford Arms Hotel in Wakefield's Bull Ring with the American singer, Tommy Roe, who had major British hits with 'Sheila' and 'The Folk Singer', trying desperately to understand his southern drawl. On another night, I recall being particularly taken by Billie Davis who had a speaking part on Mike Sarne's 'Will I What?' and her own big hit with 'Tell Him'. Her striking looks and friendliness when signing her autograph made a big impression on us spotty adolescents.

Sarne had been due to appear at one concert, closing the first half of a show that was headed, I think, by John Leyton of 'Johnny Remember Me' fame, and who also acted in the film *The Great Escape*. But, for some reason, he pulled out of the tour just before Wakefield and was replaced by an American male vocal group which, not long before, had achieved their first major success with a song called 'Sherry'. To this day, having attended the first 'house' of the show that evening, I remain convinced Wakefield staged the Four Seasons' European debut and that I was there to see it. Certainly the backing group they had that night were very obviously unfamiliar with their routine. As I recall, it was either The Outlaws or the Innocents, who were backing 'Don't You Think It's Time' singer Mike Berry, on the same tour.

Of course, the Beatles had also performed at the ABC Regal some time before their first hit 'Love Me Do', but this slightly pre-dated what, for me, became an obsession with sixties music and Helen Shapiro, the headline act with them, didn't particularly appeal. But for the rest of the period there would have been few I missed, including ex-Tornado, Heinz, of 'Just Like Eddie' fame, Lulu and Billy J. Kramer and the Dakotas.

They Walked on Water

With pals from Wakefield, I'd travel further afield for the big names. I saw the Beach Boys at Leeds Odeon. Their music, more than any other, connected directly to where I was at as a young lad in his early teens. 'When I Grow Up To Be A Man', 'She's Not The Little Girl I Once Knew' and 'In My Room', for example, resonated at the time.

With my mate Anthony 'Chris' Ellis, I was on the front row at Bradford Gaumont when the Rolling Stones performed in 1963. When they came on, dozens of screaming girls from the back of the audience ran towards the front and security staff linked arms behind our seats. I gave up mine to a girl who'd fainted in the aisle to my left and was promptly dragged to the back by a couple of heavies who thought I had been part of the dash. Sadly, 'Chris' died far too young but his twin sons inherited his great passion for music and have achieved considerable success with Wakefield band The Cribs.

The music of the sixties seemed to connect, not just to the traumas, struggles and aspirations of us adolescents, but also to horizons way beyond our world at the time. The Tornodoes' 'Telstar' epitomised, in 1962, the wonder of the space race and the mysteries of the universe yet to unfold. I bought into the drama of it in quite a big way. My parents knew the family of a Wakefield man, Ronnie Bedford, who, having started work on the local *Wakefield Express* newspaper, had made quite a name for himself in the USA as a journalist for the *Christian Science Monitor*. He specialised in reporting on space exploration and I was given an illustrated book about the subject which he had written at the time. Somehow - perhaps through him - I felt more connected to the evolving story of space exploration than most of my peers.

I'm not sure whether the content of much of the music of the sixties influenced my early political awareness but, from the 1962 Cuban missile crisis, I was certainly aware of living in a period of immense international uncertainties around the issue of the nuclear bomb, underlined constantly by many songs which reflected, particularly, the doubts of youth. Bob Dylan's 'A Hard Rain's A-Gonna Fall', recorded that year, added to our consciousness of the potential implications of nuclear war. On this side of the Atlantic, the Liverpool group the Searchers continued the anti- nuclear bomb theme in 1964 with 'What Have They Done To The Rain?'

The second half of the decade increasingly saw popular music reflecting political issues with Barry McGuire's 'Eve of Destruction', in particular, offering a devastating critique of some of the hypocrisy around nuclear weapons, the Vietnam war and racial conflict:

> *Don't you understand what I'm trying to say,*
> *Can't you feel the fears I'm feeling today?*
> *If the button is pushed, there's no runnin' away,*
> *There'll be no-one to save, with the world in a grave...*
> *You may leave here for four days in space,*
> *But when you return it's the same old place,*
> *The poundin' of the drums, the pride and disgrace,*
> *You can bury your dead, but don't leave a trace,*
> *Hate your next-door-neighbour, but don't forget to say grace...*

It's difficult to recall when my lifelong interest in politics actually began, but I was certainly politically aware by the start of the decade and, like many at the time, increasingly conscious that I was growing up in a unique era. I had delivered the news of Kennedy's assassination in 1963 to the folk of Wakefield's Thornes Road on my newspaper round, having been stunned by the announcement late during the previous evening while I was listening to the music of Radio Luxembourg. I was a firm supporter of Harold Wilson's modernisation agenda by the time of his becoming Prime Minister in 1964. It's hard to describe my joy at seeing grouse-moor Tories like Harold Macmillan and Alec Douglas-Home replaced by someone with the common touch and a Yorkshireman to boot, who came from the town where rugby league was born.

Failing the 11+ examination played a major part in my politicisation alongside having, as a child, seen my father struggle with serious illness and occasional redundancy. These events and others shaped my thinking and understanding of the remarkable political changes which were taking place nationally and internationally during the 1960s. And of course the spectre of race - never far from the surface in the US and South Africa as I was growing up - had become centre stage in British politics through Enoch Powell's infamous 'rivers of blood' speech, only days before the 1968 Cup final was due to take place.

While there was an awareness of the dangers and insecurities of the nuclear age and of the fact that the divisiveness of race was entering mainstream debate in Britain too, there was the magic of the music and a genuine sense of a bright new order in politics. But the sixties for me contained something even more special - the finest ever sustained period of success for the team I had grown up supporting. By 1968, Wakefield Trinity was part of me and I was part of it.

I had started watching Trinity during the 1956/7 season and, as soon as I was old enough, joined a group of school pals at the Belle Vue ground every home match, wearing the red and blue scarf my mother had knitted me. The sporting action and signature tunes of the times seemed to somehow coalesce as the team came on to the field at home matches accompanied by the likes of the Shadows' 'Apache'. Not only did our gang become fixtures at the ground every other Saturday afternoon but also at the team's regular training sessions on Tuesday and Thursday evenings. With other youngsters, we would congregate at the back of the old West Stand, which in those days housed the players' changing rooms, and seek autographs from them as they emerged.

This sense of something particularly 'special' was underlined at the time when Wakefield author David Storey had his novel about a fictional rugby league player, Arthur Machin, turned into the film *This Sporting Life*. Starring Richard Harris and Rachel Roberts, many of the on-field action scenes were filmed at Belle Vue and Trinity players appeared in them. The crowds shown in the film had assembled at Belle Vue for actual matches although cardboard models of spectators were used for the more sparsely attended reserve team match shots. Wakefield's famous Dolphin pub, at the junction of Warrengate and Kirkgate, where I later consumed more than a few under-age drinks while watching the 'cabaret', also featured in celluloid. The autobiography of Sammy King, the club singer, contains a wonderful description of the Dolphin (now known as the Wakey Arms) in the 1960s. He wrote, 'Run by the indestructible Tommy Fisher, it boasted criminals, homosexuals, lesbians, bisexuals, misfits, drunkards - and that was just the staff.'

Anyone living in Wakefield during 1962, when the film was being shot at various locations in the area, will have memories of the time. One of our neighbours had a rather eccentric white boxer dog called Keo which made a habit of travelling considerable distances on its own, using public transport. It had ended up in Bradford one day, having got a bus to Wakefield, boarding a train to Bradford at Westgate station. It must have got wind of important happenings at Belle Vue at the time and, although the dog lived perhaps three miles from the ground, he was found there on one occasion having disrupted the filming.

Although several school friends and I are in the crowd scenes, because it was classed as 'X' certificate, when it was shown at Wakefield's Playhouse Cinema on its release we were restricted to peering at the still shots displayed outside the entrance. We were deemed too young to be allowed to see Rachel Roberts in her bra and the bare backsides of some of the players emerging from a post-match communal bath.

This Sporting Life was a major box office success and put Wakefield, its rugby league team and the sport as a whole very much on the map nationally at the time. As a consequence, those of us at probably the most impressionable age of our lives were mightily impressed. Alongside the enormous success of Trinity on the field, with seemingly endless matches without defeat in the early 1960s, life could scarcely have been better.

So as 1968 arrived I was all but grown up but not too steeped in the adult world to be apathetic over Trinity's ongoing Challenge Cup run. I was watching the team both home and away at that time, travelling to opposing teams' grounds with mates on a Victoria Motors coach which set off from a garage at Newton Hill, on the Leeds side of the city. Trinity had a sizeable following then and, with the old South Stand at Belle Vue still in use, the younger end in particular could generate some noise from within it. There was chanting, there was singing and Bob Dylan's 'Mighty Quinn', popularised by the British group, Manfred Mann, was predictably and easily transformed into 'Mighty Trin'. Donovan's 'Mellow Yellow' was morphed into a song about Trinity full-back Gary Cooper, but it is much too far back for me to remember the words. It's hard to explain how it felt at the time, but the incredible music seemed somehow perfectly intertwined with being a fan. And the icing on the cake - the kind of culmination of the fabulous sixties - was going to Wembley for the first time.

All that was very much in the back of my mind as I found myself, all those years later, in almost surreal surroundings enjoying the hospitality of the Hebblethwaites as the match played out unerringly in front of us. The *Rugby Leaguer* produced during the week of the final gave a detailed profile of John Hebblethwaite, a York-based scientific instrument technician. It noted that during the Second World War he had played for York as a scrum-half but had turned to refereeing in 1946, passing his first whistler's examination that year. He had previously taken charge of an England-France amateur international and the paper noted that, 'as he has been on the Grade One list a dozen years…his selection as this season's Wembley referee is not in advance of time.'

John Hebblethwaite's younger son, David, maintains that when he played for York he was actually a winger. His involvement with the club arose during the War when he was exempt from the armed forces because his work as an instrument maker involved him manufacturing gun-sights. 'He was in the Home Guard, on the Knavesmire. The only time they let their gun off, they got court-martialled! It was on VE Day.'

Missing from the profile was that this was not the first time Hebblethwaite had been an official at a Wembley final. According to David, he had been a touch judge at the 1950 decider between Warrington and Widnes. 'He always cursed me, saying 'You nearly cost me a Wembley place' because I was born two days before.'

An article about his achievement, published in the *Yorkshire Evening Press* on the eve of the '68 game, indicated that John Hebblethwaite had received nearly one hundred messages, by post or telephone, congratulating him on his appointment as the man in the middle. 'They have come from clubs, from colleagues in the York Referees' Society - whose presentation silver whistle he will be using tomorrow - and from soccer referees.' Clearly, he was well thought of at the time. The Leeds hooker in the game Tony Crosby, like Hebblethwaite, hailed from York, knew him well and held him in high esteem. 'I always found him pretty fair both in the amateur game and when I was at York and Leeds. He was always a good referee I thought.'

At the time of his appointment John Hebblethwaite was Secretary of the Senior Referees Society and was shortly due to serve a second year as President of the Yorkshire County Referees' Society. He retained his interest in the amateur game and was Vice-Chairman of the York and District ARL.

David Hebblethwaite clearly recalls his father learning of his appointment to referee the 1968 final. 'He got a letter from Bill Fallowfield, who was in charge then. My dad used to work at a garage just opposite us on a night and I can remember my mam saying, "Oh. There's a letter come for your dad today. Run over to the garage with it." I took it over and he opened it there and then and he confirmed that he'd got Wembley. He was over the moon, over the moon. That is the highlight of your career, whether you're a player or a referee.' The local paper reported his reaction to the news at the time: 'To get the Wembley appointment after so many years is 'really wonderful' Mr. Hebblethwaite says. And his wife, Winifred, who travels widely with him during the season is really thrilled to be going with him to London.'

It was indeed an honour for a man who had clearly given a great deal to the sport over many years. But no-one could have anticipated just how John Hebblethwaite's role in this remarkable final would become deeply embedded in the annals of the history of the game.

Chapter Three

Not just any opponents: the sociology of a rugby league derby

On their way to the Challenge Cup final in 1968, Leeds had beaten Liverpool City, Bramley and Oldham before defeating Wigan in fine style at the penultimate stage. The performance of the team that day at Swinton was widely seen as marking the coming together of a great side which played open, attractive football, very much inspired by the coaching of Roy Francis. Wakefield had, by then, entered a glorious period, winning the Championship Trophy for the first time in the club's history the previous year. Although several of the players who had delivered Trinity three Wembley successes in the earlier years of the decade had either retired or moved on, the management had, in the main, replaced them with individuals of considerable calibre.

It is probably fair to say that Wakefield's passage to the capital involved them in some tougher assignments than Leeds had faced. They had beaten strong Barrow and Salford sides away from home, defeated Castleford at Belle Vue before drawing with Huddersfield in the semi-final at

Headingley and beating them on the same ground in the replay. Once Trinity had clinched a place at the Twin Towers, anticipation of the first cup and league double in the club's history began in earnest. In most years during that era, then, as now, the Championship final constituted the season's last match. In 1968, however, it was the Challenge Cup decider which was to wind up the season, taking place on the Saturday after the most consistent tag was decided.

As the Championship Play-offs got underway both Leeds and Wakefield were in with a chance of the elusive double. From a Trinity perspective, the joint-editors of their official programme in the issue of 24th April 1968, David Armitage and John Lindley, noted that, 'Only two sides in these post-war years have placed both these trophies together; a number have entered the final two Saturdays with a chance of both titles…some have failed in one, others have failed in both of them!'

Warrington in 1954 - both of their finals being against Halifax - and St Helens twelve years later were the supreme pair. Wakefield supporters did not need reminding that, after beating Hull at Wembley in 1960, they lost to Wigan in following week's Championship set to, or that Trinity would have landed all four of the game's major trophies (the double and the Yorkshire Cup and League) had they been able to beat Huddersfield in the 1962 Championship final as well as at Wembley the week before.

Perhaps, though, this time more than anything, was the fact that Leeds were Trinity's opponents and stood in the way of the ultimate achievement. Of all the rugby league rivalries I had grown up with, the biggest, twice a season, was the derby against Leeds. As a youngster, the first ever away match I attended, going on the Trinity supporters' bus, was at Headingley on Boxing Day. We pulled up behind the South

Stand to find that the match had been called off because of fog. But I attended many more of those clashes over the years, meeting mates, some of whom I would only see annually at this match, in the Skyrack and Original Oak pubs in Headingley. And, of course, also never to be missed were the return matches at Belle Vue, often played over the Easter period. Such was the importance of games against Leeds, that if Wakefield won one or both of them, indifferent form over the rest of the season could often be set aside.

The sociology of Wakefield supporters' attitudes to Leeds RLFC could, and perhaps should, be the subject of serious academic study. Any attempt to understand the feelings and reactions to the outcome of Wembley '68 from a Wakefield perspective has to take full account of the fact that the perceived gross injustices and tragedies of that day didn't just occur against any team. They were against Leeds.

I know of few witnesses to the intense rivalry better able to put them into words than life-long Trinity supporter, Gerry Wright. Like myself, he accompanied his father to Belle Vue for the first time around 1956 and has been faithfully following Wakefield through thick and thin ever since. An occupant of the East Stand, Wright's regular half-time match analyses to the assembled throng adjacent to the gents' toilet to the rear of the stand is still the stuff of legend. Fire and brimstone would be an understatement. Were they to be delivered downstairs in the home team's dressing room the players surely wouldn't have dared to fail to perform in the second half. At the end of any home match his loudly expressed - almost broadcast - opinions on performance have been known to cause alarm to the bewildered, now largely Asian, occupants of St. Catherine's Street as he returns to his car.

Wright, more than most, can explain how Trinity supporters' attitudes to Leeds have passed down through the generations. 'Now, my father was a reasonable soul, really, until he started on about Leeds,' he remembers. 'Most people regarded him as a good egg, a God-fearing man, conscientious worker, ordinary working class bloke, man of sobriety and everything, but get him onto Leeds and he seemed to take on a Jekyll and Hyde sort of existence.'

Wright recalls clearly how his father influenced him in respect of these matters. 'As a child, he regaled me with tales about Leeds and how they bought up everybody's best players in the 1930s, but particularly when teams were financially embarrassed, and Wakefield were often financially embarrassed. Sir Edwin Airey was the [Leeds] chairman and had this phrase - 'Go get me that man'. And they finished with a crackerjack team in the 1930s, with Eric Harris and some other top Australians. But I recall my father's anger at the loss of Stanley Smith - a Test wingman - and Alf Watson, who was a loose forward of great ability, two produced by Wakefield Trinity in the 1930s who were poached by Leeds. There were others - people like Charlie Glossop who, in the sixties, was a committee man at Trinity.'

Wright Senior's account of the source of his attitude to Leeds is similar to many from subsequent generations of Wakefield supporters. Gerry Wright, like me, suffered the transfer of outstanding Great Britain forward Don Robinson from Trinity to Leeds even though we were children in the 1950s. And in the years that followed - although obviously there was two-way movement - the trend has fairly consistently been exactly that outlined by Gerry's father, with Wakefield's best ending up at Headingley. Indeed, not long after the 1968 final, two of Trinity's forwards that day, Bob Haigh and David Jeanes, both of whom became internationals, donned the blue and amber. There were many others, right down to the transfer of Gareth Ellis, which has probably informed the thinking of my children's generation of Wakefield supporters. The simple fact is that Leeds have always had the cheque book and Trinity usually needed the money.

Gerry Wright says, 'All this, I was socialised into and it was in my consciousness and probably still is. My father considered Leeds the main team to beat and, like many of his generation, Leeds/Trinity clashes were more important than any other game. I think he resented Leeds more than he liked Trinity. He once said to me - and this is the truth - he would buy a Leeds season ticket if it could be guaranteed they'd lose every home match. My mother often thought he was a little bit over the top but, nonetheless, he did get very passionate about Leeds and Wakefield Trinity.'

There were other perceived disparities arising from Leeds being the larger adjoining city which entrenched attitudes towards Leeds RLFC. Gerry Wright suggests 'Leeds had all the swagger of a big city club, backed by a biased local evening press. Wakefield never had its own evening paper so often we either read the *Yorkshire Evening News* or the *Yorkshire Evening Post*. Whenever they covered rugby league games they always carried the Leeds scorers, when they were playing home and away, in capital letters. To sensitive people, or people like my father, this was even more of a red rag to a bull.'

To appreciate, perhaps, why 1968 has remained deep within the psyche of generations of Wakefield folk it is important to understand that the perspectives from as far back as the 1920s and 1930s remain, for many, just as relevant today. Gerry Wright makes a very fair point that Trinity's contemporary rivalry with Castleford has more relevance now than it used to but, to most Trinity followers, Leeds remain the real enemy.

The fact that, in recent times, Trinity have found themselves fighting with Castleford over scraps from the Super League table has had a bearing on how they currently perceive each other and the tensions around the longstanding struggle of both clubs to deliver new stadia has added to local rivalries. The use of evidence from Castleford's then Chief Executive, Richard Wright, which questioned Wakefield Trinity's need for a new stadium at the planning inquiry into the proposed Newmarket development, during December 2010, caused one or two ripples.

Wakefield and Castleford, part of the same local government area since 1974, have, compared to Leeds, far more that unites them as communities than divides them. Both suffered badly as a consequence of the pit closure programme during the 1980s and early 1990s and the dependence of their wider economies on the coal industry meant that both areas have had a long, hard struggle to recover. Leeds, on the other hand, with a much more diverse economic base, not only survived the bitter realities of the Thatcher era, but evolved subsequently into one of the country's most prosperous major cities.

So, in some senses, the big city 'swagger' identified in the relationship between Trinity and Leeds is as relevant now as it ever was. From a Wakefield perspective there remains a perception that Leeds is always trying to put a spanner in the works and prevent their neighbour succeeding. The fact that objections from Leeds City Council to the development of the Newmarket site for the new Trinity stadium lead to planning approval being 'called in' by the Government was seen, by some, as just one more example. Indeed, those objections lead directly to Wakefield Trinity going into administration and, although undoubtedly the club has emerged stronger as a consequence, the factors leading to it and the implications of delays in the construction of the new stadium because of the subsequent planning inquiry, will not be forgotten by many Wakefield supporters.

I would be willing to wager a bet that the Wakefield supporters of today - most of whom were probably not around in 1968 - would overwhelmingly gain far more genuine joy over beating Leeds than any other team in Super League. A miserable season in the lower reaches of the table can be tolerated, if not enjoyed, if the record shows that Leeds were beaten at least once. And, while the Trinity team of the sixties were a much greater power in the land than they are at the time of writing, as the 1968 Challenge Cup final was anticipated, the age-old enmity could not be underestimated, at least as far as Wakefield supporters were concerned.

Chapter Four

Setting the scene

Looking back at the 1968 final nearly four and a half decades later it is very apparent that rugby league has changed in a number of significant ways. Firstly, to understand the nature of the game on that wet day at Wembley it has to be appreciated that the rules which applied then were significantly different to those of today. Perhaps the most important difference was that the game was played under a four-tackle rule, rather than the six allowed now.

The change from unlimited tackles had taken place in 1966 in an attempt to make the game more attractive at a time when there was genuine concern over declining attendances. It was generally accepted that this final brought together British rugby league's two top teams but the declining support base of both at the time clearly justified this concern. Wakefield's average crowd that season - when the side, for the second year running, had won the title - was 5,982, down from 7,205 just two years earlier. At a 6,825 average for the 1967/68 season, Leeds were down from just over 8,000 during the previous year. While there are people who criticise attendances in 2013, it is worth noting that, having come out of administration and started last season with an almost entirely new squad, Wakefield's average attendance during 2012 was nearer 8,000 while Leeds' was more than double that of 1967/68.

The rule change of 1966 reflected a desire to end a monopoly on possession by one side. At the end of the tackle count, if the ball wasn't kicked by the attacking side, a scrum was formed giving the defending team the opportunity to gain the ball. Consequently, at the time of the '68 final, significantly more scrumaging took place during a game and, they were properly contested which meant that many sides chose to include specialists in the art, particularly at hooker and prop.

The distance between attack and defence was five yards, rather than the ten metres which applies nowadays, and there was no 40-20 rule, where 'head and ball' in the subsequent scrum is awarded to the attacking side if it successfully kicks indirectly into touch from their own half to within their opponents twenty metre area. In contrast to the four substitutes and ten interchanges of the modern game, back then, the Rugby Football League had, only three seasons earlier, followed the Australians in permitting two substitutes who, at the time of this match, could only be used to replace injured players before half-time. And, of course, one major difference between that final and the televised matches of today was that the referee did not have the replay technology and big screen which is so often used to determine crucial decisions. At least in Wakefield circles, speculation continues to this day as to what would have been the outcome had there been.

The second major difference concerns the personnel of

the two competing sides that day. It is quite striking how, compared to the modern game, both of them contained a significant number of players local to the Leeds and Wakefield areas. Although it must be acknowledged that the Rhinos' recent triumphs have contained a core of Academy-raised products, in Syd Hynes, Barry Seabourne and the Eyre brothers, Leeds had four players who had even been to the same school - Bewerley Street County Primary in Hunslet. In contrast with teams which are nowadays peppered with Australians and New Zealanders, in particular, only one foreign player - Wakefield's Gert Coetzer, a South African - featured at Wembley.

The Leeds team that day included at full-back Bev Risman, son of rugby league true great, Gus Risman, who had signed professional terms for Leigh after playing for the England Rugby Union team at fly half. He had joined Leeds in early 1966 and had been the sport's top goal-kicker during the 1966/67 season with 163. He had played for Great Britain in their wins against France earlier in the season and, after Neil Fox's withdrawal, had been chosen as captain of the Great Britain team for the World Championship series. The *Yorkshire Evening Post*'s souvenir brochure, produced before the final, interestingly noted the occupation of only one of the 26 players whose pen pictures were included. Risman, it said, was a 'Schoolmaster.' Perhaps the significance of his occupation, at a time when players were overwhelmingly involved in manual trades, was deemed worthy of note.

On the right wing was Alan Smith, who had signed in 1962 from the Wakefield amateur side, Brookhouse and established himself in the first team earlier in the season when regular winger, Ron Cowan, was injured. His centre partner was Syd Hynes, who had initially played rugby league with Hunslet Schools but had been signed by Leeds after playing union with Leeds NALGO. The left-centre was Bernard Watson who had previously captained the England Amateur Rugby League side and joined Leeds in 1964 from the junior club, Thornhill, near Dewsbury. Watson's wing partner was John Atkinson who had signed in 1965 from Roundhay Rugby Union club.

Loiners' half-back partners were Mick Shoebottom and Barry Seabourne. Stand-off Shoebottom had originally come to Headingley as a scrum-half from the Bisons Sports junior outfit in the city. He had, by the time of the final, made a number of county appearances and was in the Great Britain squad for the World Championships. Scrum-half Seabourne had captained the Hunslet Schools team and made his debut for Leeds at the age of 16. He had by then been selected to represent Yorkshire.

The Leeds open-side prop and captain was Mick Clark, who had played with Dewsbury, Huddersfield and Salford before coming to Headingley in 1963. Like Risman, he had appeared for Great Britain in the wins against France and was also in the World Championship squad. Hooker Tony Crosby had signed from York in 1966 and taken over from Alan Lockwood in the first team earlier in the year. At blind-side prop was Ken Eyre who had previously played for Hunslet in the famous Wembley final against Wigan in 1965 and been capped for Great Britain against New Zealand that same year.

Eyre's brother, Albert, was in the second row and, at the age of 16 had been expected to sign for Hunslet for what was then a standard £25 fee. But, according to the younger Eyre, his father had told Hunslet officials, 'You don't think you're going to get two out of t'same belly for £50.' Albert Eyre signed instead for Keighley for £600 and played with them for eight seasons before coming to Leeds in 1967. His partner in the second-row was Bill Ramsey, another product of

Hunslet schools and junior football, who had like Ken Eyre, played at Wembley in 1965. He toured Australasia in 1966 with Great Britain and was the highest valued Leeds player with his transfer from Hunslet costing £10,000. The 'last man down' in blue and amber was Ray Batten who came from a family which had produced several very talented rugby league players. Originally from York he played for the Heworth local amateur side and had signed for Leeds early in 1963.

The Leeds reserves on the day were Normanton born, John Langley, in his first full season at Headingley, and Mick Joyce, like Alan Smith, a product of Brookhouse, who had been with Leeds since 1962.

Opposing them, Trinity's full-back in the final was Gary Cooper who, as a Featherstone Rovers player, had toured Australasia with Great Britain - as a centre - in 1962. He had transferred to Wakefield after a dispute with Rovers at the start of the 1967/8 season. On the right-wing was Ken Hirst who, after playing league with Leeds schools, had joined Wakefield from Morley Rugby Union Club in 1956 at the age of 16.

Selected at right-centre was Ian Brooke who had come through Trinity's nursery and played in the 1963 final against Wigan. He had transferred to Bradford Northern in 1964 but returned to Wakefield in early '67. Brooke had toured Australasia in 1966 and played in all the five international matches during the '68 season. With Neil Fox absent from the side due to injury, a massive blow not least as the game's greatest-ever point's scorer, his left-centre birth was taken by South African, Gert Coetzer, normally a left-winger. He had played for the Bloemfontein Aquilas before joining Trinity in February, 1963. Within three months of his arrival he had scored two tries at Wembley in his side's triumph over

Wigan. In Coetzer's usual left-wing role that day was Ken Batty who had joined Wakefield in 1965 from rugby union club, West Park in Leeds. At the time of the final he was Wakefield's top try-scorer.

The Wakefield half-backs were Harold Poynton and Ray Owen. Stand-off Poynton was the skipper. A product of Wakefield Schools, he had joined the club in 1958 and played at Wembley in 1962 and the following year, when he won the Lance Todd Trophy. He had toured Australia with Great Britain in 1962 and skippered Trinity's first-ever Championship winning side in 1967, lifting the trophy again the following year. Scrum-half Owen had signed from Widnes during the 1964/65 season but had been out of action for a considerable time in the run-up to Wembley. Consequently, Trinity had signed Joe Bonnar from Whitehaven as cover but he had injury problems and Owen returned in time for the 1968 Championship play-offs.

David Jeanes, who had signed for Trinity from Wakefield Rugby Union club at the start of the 1967/68 season, was open-side prop, with George Shepherd at hooker. Shepherd, who played internationally at under-19 level had joined Trinity in early 1964 and gained first team selection after Geoff Oakes suffered a broken leg in a home league win against St. Helens. At blind-side prop was Don Fox who, after a distinguished career as a scrum-half with Featherstone Rovers, came to Trinity during 1965, moving to loose-forward and eventually into the front-row. Among his representative honours, Fox had been a Great Britain tourist in 1962.

While I had grown up hero-worshipping his brother Neil, by the time of the 1968 final Don had become firmly fixed as my favourite Trinity player. From the time I could first kick a goal from in front of the posts at Lawefield Lane Primary School I had always insisted that I played 'Foxy' in our childhood games but only had a vague notion of the existence of two older Fox brothers. Although I had seen Don play for Featherstone, his arrival at Belle Vue had impressed upon me what a wonderfully skilled player he was. In my late teens I still had somewhat unrealistic ambitions to make it as a player and I could associate myself more with someone who wasn't as big as Neil or, by any means, the fastest of players. Although I trained regularly at the time, my Friday and Saturday nights in the pubs of Wakefield were starting to show on the waistline and an added affinity with Don was that, towards the end of his marvellous career, he was also showing just a bit of a paunch.

Like Joe Bonnar, Trinity second-row Matt McLeod had joined the club from Whitehaven shortly before the 1967/8 season's cup register closed and had played at county level for Cumberland. He was partnered by another product of the Belle Vue nursery, Bob Haigh, who had signed professional terms at the club in 1962. By the time of the final, Haigh had already gained selection for the Great Britain squad in the World Championship. Another local product was selected at loose-forward. David Hawley had signed for Trinity as a hooker in 1966 but had settled at number 13 after Fox had moved to prop.

Trinity's reserves that day, who were to take no part in the match, were David Garthwaite and Gerry Round. Garthwaite, a three-quarter, had signed professional terms from Wakefield Rugby Union Club at the start of the 1965/6 season while Round was a veteran of the 1960, '62 and '63 finals. Although an established full-back in these matches, by the cup run six years later he had moved to play in the forwards.

Team coaches back in the sixties gained far less attention than they do nowadays. But it is worth noting that, in discussing this match with many of the surviving players who took part, it was very evident there was far more emphasis from the Leeds players on the role and importance of their factotum, Roy Francis, than, from the Wakefield players on the contribution of Ken Traill.

I knew neither of them but gain the distinct impression that they were very different people, with significantly differing approaches to the job. Like several of the Leeds side, Ken Traill was a Hunslet lad but he made his name as a player with Bradford Northern. After an inauspicious debut, when he had to leave the field early, suffering from sunstroke, Traill had established himself as an outstanding loose-forward, winning nine Great Britain caps. Trevor Foster, who played in the same Bradford side in the late 1940s and early '50s, held him in the highest regard. 'He was a tremendous player with a wonderful kicking game. He was probably the best passer of the ball I have ever seen,' he told the *Independent* in 2002.

Traill's appearance in the film *This Sporting Life* was referred to in Dave Hadfield's obituary of him in that same article in which he made the point that the 'old head' role he had played in the film, showing Richard Harris how to approach the game, 'was a role he had often played in real life.' Foster's view of him was that 'He was very popular and, off the field, very quiet. But he didn't suffer mediocre players gladly. His principle was nothing but the best.'

From around 1958, when Traill began coaching Trinity, my position with my mates at Belle Vue, was directly to the side of the Wakefield dug-out at the front of the terrace by the old West Stand. The players' changing rooms were under it in those days. We held a much envied position, requiring the occupants to be in place probably an hour and a half before kick-off to be sure of gaining the spot. Its attractions were that we were privy to the comings and goings of the dug-out, had a good view of the bust noses and lips, and could clearly hear the dialogue between the bench and players. Coming from a non-smoking, teetotal and definitely no-swearing household, I can honestly say that Ken Traill made a significant contribution to the completion of my education. He may, as Foster has suggested, have been quiet away from the game, but in that dug-out, if things weren't going Trinity's way, it would be an understatement to say that he would turn the air blue. But his methods clearly delivered success. The 1968 final represented a seventh, record-setting visit to Wembley as a player and coach.

I wasn't in any way privy to a similar close up view of Roy Francis but the picture I have gained of him from those who knew him is of someone who probably had a rather different approach. One clear and consistent theme in the discussion of Wembley '68, is the admiration of the Leeds players for his contribution. Everyone I have spoken to has referred to the significance of his role in terms of the success of the Leeds side at that time and most have mentioned, in particular, his pre-match motivational team talk on the morning before that final.

Francis was a rugby league convert, originating from Wales, who had previously been with Wigan, Barrow, Warrington and Hull and had coached Hull's losing side at Wembley on two previous occasions, in 1959 and 1960. In his *Illustrated History of Rugby League*, Robert Gate remarks of his time with Leeds, that, 'Under far-sighted coach Roy Francis, the Loiners played exhilarating open football which delighted the eye. Players such as John Atkinson, Syd Hynes, Bev Risman, Alan Smith, Ron Cowan, Mick Shoebottom, Barry Seabourne, Mick Clark, Bill Ramsey and Ray Batten became masters of the new [limited-tackle] style game.'

Barry Seabourne, even now, cannot overstate his estimation of Francis, his methods and approach. 'He was miles ahead of his day - today's coach - in his forward way of thinking. Now, the game is basically speed and power but his game was speed and playing rugby. We worked a lot on speed. We did a lot of sprinting.' Ken Rollin remarks that Francis was, 'a little beyond the others as a coach. His enthusiasm was incredible. All he wanted to do was make a good Leeds team and he did. I thought he was a fantastic coach.' Rollin was in a good position to compare Francis with Trinity's coach Ken Traill. 'Ken,' he says, 'was slightly different. He was very good at selecting new players, for example, Derek Turner, Don Vines, etc.'

Ken Eyre highlights Francis's role in the development of some of the players in that 1968 side. 'John Atkinson, maybe two years before, was scoring half a dozen tries [a season] in the 'A' team. Roy sort of took him in hand. Alan Smith - I wasn't there at the time - had been sent to Bramley. He came back to Headingley and they became the two outstanding wingers of their time.' Alan Smith was, by 1968, challenging for a regular first team place and he remembers Francis telling him to closely observe the player he was competing with for the Leeds right wing position. 'I was only just established and thinking I'm not really ready for this. Roy used to say 'Just look at that Ronnie Cowan, how gracefully he runs.' Roy coached everybody individually. He got the best out of everyone. He was like the Pied Piper and all the young kids loved him. He got everybody singing from the same hymn sheet, thinking he was wonderful.'

Atkinson pinpoints Roy Francis and Johnny Whiteley as the two best coaches he ever played for. 'They never taught you how to play rugby because they said "You're good enough to be in my side. I don't need to teach you how to play." Basically they motivated you and both of them were fitness fanatics. All our training at Headingley [under Francis] was sprinting, basically, on the cricket field. And everybody had to be as fast as they possibly could, and that included the props, everybody. If you went through a gap, you could run and somebody would get to you.' Alan Smith says Francis would mark out the cricket field for the sprinting sessions. 'We'd do 800 yards as fast as we could against the clock. Then he'd wind it down to 400 and then to 200.'

Tony Crosby also recalls his coach's emphasis on speed. 'Roy Francis wasn't all that tactical. His view was pass the ball along the line and let's get it quicker. We didn't have a lot of moves either, possibly two with Ray Batten, then Atki and Smithy coming round the scrum. He was a man of fitness and straight forward stuff.'

Ken Eyre says, 'I knew Roy Francis was an excellent trainer and coach, from playing against his Hull teams. Joining him at Leeds was a bit daunting at times because we didn't see eye to eye straightaway, but we did eventually. I got over my problems after Roy and I sat down and had a long talk. One of the things we spoke about [was] I didn't think I was playing the football that I was brought up to play. And Roy sorted me out. One of the things I put to him was why did we have all these old players?' At this point, a significant number of the Leeds first team were towards the end of their careers. Ken Eyre continues, 'He said, 'I bought time.' He knew that Barry Seabourne was going to be an arch-schemer. He knew that Mick Shoebottom was a powerhouse.'

Chapter Five

Selection issues

Bearing in mind that it is now an annual convention for most Super League coaches to criticise their team being required to play two matches over the Easter weekend, it is worth noting that, as they approached their Championship final clash with Hull Kingston Rovers a week before Wembley, Wakefield Trinity had actually played nine matches in 29 days. Commenting on the seven day break the players got before the first of the two finals, Trinity's Don Fox was reported in the *Yorkshire Evening Post* saying 'It's been like a holiday.'

Inevitably, the intensity of the programme had taken its toll in terms of injuries. A home match against St. Helens had seen hooker Geoff Oakes break his leg and Neil Fox sustain a groin injury which caused him to miss all but one of those nine matches. Oakes' key hooking role was initially to have been taken on by veteran Bernard Prior returning to action but he had sustained a thigh muscle injury and George Shepherd took over in the middle of the engine room. Scrum-half Ray Owen had been troubled by injuries earlier in the season but returned to action for the play-off matches.

The most significant worry for Wakefield concerned the fitness of their international goal-kicking left centre Neil Fox. Talismanic Fox remembers '68 as a great year for him. 'It started off well because I was captain of Great Britain and we went over to France and won and came back here and did likewise. That was an achievement at that time. And in between these matches, Bill Fallowfield and the Rugby Football League arranged games with Salford, Halifax and Leeds, keeping the Great Britain team together because they were preparing for the World Cup.'

Fox, during this period, was clearly facing problems in respect of his match fitness. 'I was struggling a little bit with the groin injury but I kept on going and doing as much as I could because I wanted to be captain of the Great Britain World Cup team in Australia.' Incredibly, the match between the Great Britain team and Halifax was arranged for the evening before Wakefield's Championship final against Hull KR and Fox turned out, playing just part of the game.

Fox had been in and out of the Wakefield team because he was resting his groin. 'That rearrangement really annoyed me but I knew that I had to play for Great Britain to prove that I was alright for the World Cup. I came off at half-time and after the match I must have rung somebody at Wakefield Trinity and said, 'I can't play tomorrow in the Championship final, my groin's been strained again. I won't be fit and I won't do justice to myself.' Anyway, the word was from the club that if I didn't play I wouldn't the week after at Wembley. So that really upset me.'

So who at Trinity would have made such a decision about the club's star player? Fox believes it would have been the club chairman and committee. 'I think if they had asked

Ken Traill, I think he would have said, 'he'll know he isn't fit' and he would have stuck by me. But I think it was the committee who were trying to show their authority. With forcing me to play, the groin went so I did miss Wembley and I also missed going to the World Cup.'

Although he had already achieved a huge amount in his career at Wakefield, Fox clearly regrets how the club treated him just before the Cup final. 'I'd never played in a World Cup. I'd been overlooked twice and, being captain of this team, I was a little bit upset with Trinity. I thought they would let me play at Wembley because I'd been there three times and picked up a winners' medal' And, as though it were an omen for what was to come, Wakefield's loss was Leeds' gain. Their full back, Bev Risman was named Great Britain skipper in Fox's place and winger, John Atkinson, was called into the squad.

As Fox was in Leeds seeing a specialist regarding his injury on the Monday before Wembley, that night's *Yorkshire Evening Post* had a photograph of the Leeds centre, Syd Hynes, their major injury worry, training with his right arm in a sling underneath his jersey. He had suffered some sort of blood clot after a kick on his bicep in a match against Widnes the previous month and the Leeds Chairman, Jack Myerscough, claimed he had a 50-50 chance of playing. Hynes says he had actually broken his arm. 'I had it in plaster for a short time but they took the plaster off and strapped it. But I was still training with the boys to keep my fitness up. On the day of the game they took the strapping off. The physio straightened my arm so I could have about three-quarters use - like a half-bend - then they strapped it round the joint so I could play at Wembley.'

Listening to the recollections of the players involved, it is difficult to avoid the conclusion that it was not unusual for them to turn out in key matches of particular importance to their clubs, when they were far from fully fit. Hynes was an important member of the Leeds squad at the time and they clearly wanted him at Wembley despite the ongoing effects of a quite significant injury. He gives the clear impression that his coach Roy Francis was prepared to risk playing him even though he would, perhaps, be restricted in terms of his contribution. 'He knew what I could do because I'd had a good season that year,' Hynes notes.

In many instances it may well have been the case that the players themselves were prepared to take the risk of playing when less than healthy, particularly when the money was on. Mick Morgan, in the early stages of his rugby league career, was part of the Trinity squad which went to Wembley and says that Gert Coetzer was far from fit when he took part. 'We faced Castleford in the quarter-final of the Championship, which I played in, and Coetzer was in the centre and he dislocated his collar-bone. He swore Paddy Armour [the Wakefield physio] to secrecy. So he played after that, all up to the end of the season, with his shoulder out. Paddy Armour - who'd seen Turner, Briggsy [Brian Briggs] and Vinesy [Don Vines] and all of them - always said he was the hardest man he'd ever see play rugby league. Gert Coetzer played at Wembley and in the Championship final. But he never played again after that. It did him.'

Bearing in mind Coetzer's subsequent role - alleged or otherwise - in the most controversial incident at Wembley, it is interesting to learn that he, too, perhaps should not have been playing. Morgan's, as a youngster with some limited first team experience, would have been keeping a close eye on the injury situation in case the opportunity arose for him to play in London.

With Neil Fox likely to be out he recalls, 'There was me,

David Garthwaite and Richard Paley, all with a chance of playing, and Kenny Batty of course. I was on the fringes, thereabouts, and obviously, with Foxy getting injured and them moving Coetzer into the centre, there was a wing spot. Even though I wasn't a winger, you thought you'd got a chance. But it was not to be. He [Ken Traill] went with Kenny Batty and David Garthwaite and Gerry Round subbed.

'Even though you knew in your heart you were a bit part player and probably weren't going to be risked at nineteen, I was obviously disappointed. I remember Trailly saying "Listen young 'un. You've plenty of time." But it never happened. So I always tell anybody - especially kids - there is no time like the present.'

Also on the Monday before, the *Yorkshire Evening Post* reported that Trinity's Don Fox had had two stitches in a lip wound incurred in the Headingley match against Hull K.R. - 'his second mouth injury in a few weeks' - but that he would be fit for Wembley. Fox's son, Greg, who was just four years old at the time, has no recollection of that but does remember what was probably the first of these two injuries. 'He came home from a semi-final and he'd lost his front teeth. He was a marked man and they didn't have the protection with the cameras that they do today. They'd tried to get him off the field but didn't succeed.'

While the intensity of Wakefield's playing commitments in the run up to the Championship final were a cause of concern, Leeds faced the problem of a lack of on-field action as the Wembley date neared. Having been eliminated from the play-offs nearly a fortnight earlier, coach Roy Francis subjected his charges to full training sessions on the Monday, Tuesday and Wednesday of the week prior to the final. Over at Belle Vue, having played two Championship games since Leeds last had a match, Trinity had a light training session on the Monday, with a further session on the Tuesday and the day off on Wednesday according to the *Evening Post*.

The media pundits were generally of the view that it would be a closely fought match between two sides capable of playing extremely attractive football. Writing in the previous Saturday's *Yorkshire Evening Post*, Arthur Haddock, who had tipped Trinity to win the Cup as far back as the first round, wrote that around half of the 32 finals played at Wembley since 1929 had been close battles '…but on no occasion did the participants look better matched than Leeds and Wakefield Trinity…'

Eddie Waring, the *Sunday Mirror*'s Rugby League columnist as well as BBC commentator, also noted how evenly matched the two side were and suggested that 'Pick your own team and give me the odds' was the punters' verdict on the match, with 5-4 either side. He came to the prophetic conclusion that, '…it is a game which, as likely as not, could be decided by a little bit of luck one way or the other…' The *Sunday Express*'s Jack Paul predicted a Leeds win but added, 'Whichever way it goes these two grand teams should provide a football feast, and I do not expect there to be many points in it.' Jack Wood, writing in the *Yorkshire Evening Press*, reckoned that the match could be a classic and, although he also predicted Leeds to win suggested, accurately, that, 'The margin will probably not be large, and a momentary slip by either side could prove a decisive factor.'

Chapter Six

Down to London

Both teams left the north for London on the Thursday of Wembley week. Wakefield had chosen to travel by train from Westgate station and the Trinity party included 22 players as well as officials. The departure day coincided with polling day in the local elections and a day off for many local youngsters as their schools were closed. The press reported that in Wakefield, '…they turned out with autograph books and enthusiastically greeted each player as he arrived at the station.' If the kids had been hoping to catch a glimpse of the Championship trophy they would have been disappointed as it did not accompany the team south. Trinity's Chairman, John Ridge, said it would be picked up on Monday evening for the procession from the station to a civic reception at the Town Hall.

Mick Morgan says that the Trinity players passed the time on the train journey playing a card game called 'Shoot' which was popular at the time. It's not clear who the winners were but Morgan remembers that Geoff Oakes was a quite spectacular loser. 'Going down he lost £180. It was a hell of a lot of money then.'

Leeds travelled on a Wallace Arnold coach, going south along the A1. As they left Headingley, their Chairman, Jack Myerscough said, 'We are going with a quiet confidence. We have had an excellent season and would like to crown it by winning the Cup. It would do the club a tremendous amount of good.' According to coach, Roy Francis, it would be, '...the icing on the cake.'

The Loiners were based on the Thursday and Friday nights at the Crystal Palace Sports Centre in London which offered good training facilities as well as accommodation. These preparatory arrangements clearly impressed the Leeds players. John Atkinson describes it as incredible. 'It was the first time we'd been to Crystal Palace, the sports centre. We'd never seen anything like it, it was absolutely unbelievable. What a brilliant idea to go there. I think it was Roy Francis who got the information about it. We were walking about with our mouths open. The nearest I'd ever experienced was Carnegie College in Leeds because my school backed on to it and you could use the track. But I'd never seen anything as professionally done as at Crystal Palace.'

Alan Smith says the Leeds players used spikes to sprint-train at the time. 'Everybody had spikes, even the forwards. Spikes were unheard of in rugby at the time.' Like Atkinson, he also was particularly impressed with staying at Crystal Palace. 'There was a tartan track, the first one, I think, in the country. Roy set us up with relay races and we'd be off like the clappers. The track was terrific. We met Geoff Capes who was training there at the same time. He was a giant of a man.' Policeman and budgie expert Capes was an England and Great Britain shot-putter, twice Commonwealth Champion, twice European Champion and a three times Olympian.

Ken Eyre recalls that they stayed in the accommodation which was used to house the athletes. It was, he says, 'a very impressive place. They were, like, apartments where you'd have a bedroom for two or three.' Barry Seabourne says their time at Crystal Place involved, 'just basic routine preparation for the game. We always trained on a Thursday so what we normally did then we carried over to the Friday. It was just preparation and working on what Wakefield's big points were and their weaknesses as well.'

Having played some 250 first team games for Trinity, Ken Rollin had signed for Leeds in 1965 and, although his career was coming to an end by 1968, Roy Francis included him in the Leeds squad for Wembley even though he had not played in any of the previous rounds. He recalls that Francis said to him, 'You've really helped over the past two and a half years. I want you to go with the squad to London.'

Obviously, Rollin had detailed knowledge of many in the Wakefield squad, an advantage of which Francis would have been well aware. Rollin also had previous Wembley experience to pass on, particularly to the younger members of the Leeds squad and, it seems, as they trained at Crystal Palace, that he was anxious about the approach being taken by some of them as they prepared for the big match. He remembers having to remind them, 'When you're going to play at Wembley you've got to put some great effort into training at this stage.' He continued, 'I felt some of the Leeds players were just having a bit of a laugh in a way. I said this is very important and was having a right go.' He left them with the warning, 'When you leave from this training session, that's it. It's then Wembley.'

Wakefield used Queens Park Rangers' Loftus Road ground for a training session on the Thursday. Ian Brooke recalls that, after they had done their rugby training, the

Wakefield players had a game of soccer on the Rangers pitch. 'The lads from QPR were watching us and one of the guys wanted to sign Harold Poynton because he was so good at football, which was amazing! We had a full length pitch. It was just something - rather than rugby - to get you in the right frame of mind, being relaxed but focused. It's hard to explain but it took your mind off the game.'

In contrast to Roy Francis's use of Ken Rollin's knowledge, Neil Fox recalls that Trinity coach Ken Traill, didn't seem to want to avail himself of the GB skipper's detailed knowledge of playing at Wembley and of some of the Leeds players. He reveals that at QPR, 'Ken only wanted the players and reserves selected along with the backroom staff in the dressing room. He asked me and Geoff Clarkson and Steeley [Geoff Steele] not to come in. 'Just go for a walk and come back in an hour's time'we were told so I didn't feel part of the team at all. Because of my experience of playing at Wembley I could have helped lads like Gert Coetzer, who came in to play in my position at centre. I could have given him some advice on how Syd Hynes and Watson played, and also Atkinson and Smith on the wings. But Ken didn't want us to be involved, so I was like a fish out of water.'

Leeds paid the traditional Friday visit to Wembley stadium to see the facilities. Tony Crosby had been there before as a spectator but had not been on the field. 'It's overpowering, even when you stand in the middle with no crowd. You just don't realise how big the stadium is. When it's empty and you're looking round that's when you feel it.'

John Atkinson had been to Wembley before, the first time in 1957 when his uncle George Broughton was playing, also on the wing for Leeds. 'I'd never been out on the pitch. We walked out and it was awe-inspiring. I can always remember what people were saying about the Wembley turf.

It was as if it should have been outside the Pope's palace in the Vatican, his lawn, because it was so brilliant. There was always this pride about Wembley's grass. The rugby pitches up north weren't the same.' On reflection, Atkinson adds, 'Of course, it was the surface that caused us all the trouble, because the rain, when it did come on the Saturday, didn't go down through the grass. It lay on top of it.'

Barry Seabourne, although a Hunslet fan as a child, had also gone to the Leeds versus Barrow final in '57, along with his school friend Syd Hynes and their parents. He too felt the majesty of the surroundings in the lead up. 'There was atmosphere even though there were no people in the ground. You could feel the tension starting to build for the day after. The pitch was lovely, it was solid.' But there had been rain earlier in the week and Hynes remembers that there were people working to drain it when they visited. 'They were still forking the pitch to get the rain away. I've got a photograph of me being on the Wembley turf on the Friday with a pitchfork with the groundsman stood at the side of me.'

Like Atkinson, Hynes and Seabourne, Alan Smith's first visit to Wembley was in 1957 when he attended with a friend and his parents. As a Wakefield lad he had then been there supporting Trinity for their three appearances in the early sixties and it is clear that there was genuine disappointment that his first on-field appearance was to be against his own. 'It was a fantastic experience but, personally, I was conflicting with this 'What am I doing here against my favourite team?' There were mixed emotions. On the Friday, driving to Wembley, there were nerves. To walk on to that pitch was unbelievable. The stadium was empty. The pitch was like a bowling green and you're in the middle of it and it seemed strangely small. We stood in the middle and I thought the posts looked near. It almost looked square to me.'

Having played at Wembley for Trinity in the 1960 final, Ken Rollin, now with the Leeds squad, was less impressed with the state of the pitch. 'I can remember going on the turf in 1960 and it was absolutely fabulous. In '68, it didn't look so good. I think there had been some horse show on it prior to the final.'

Ken Eyre had played there with Hunslet in 1965 staying at the Baileys Hotel where Trinity were booked this time. Three years earlier, it had actually been Wakefield's Secretary-Manager Eddie Thomas who had chosen the hotel as it had been expected that Trinity would defeat Hunslet in the semi-final. But they lost and the Hunslet squad took over the booking. Having been before, Eyre determined that, after spending much of the Thursday on the bus, he would give Wembley a miss. Despite the importance of the occasion, he gives the impression that he didn't exactly relish a departure from his normal, weekly, match regime. 'My style of getting ready for the match was to report three-quarters of an hour before the game, read the programme, twenty-five to three start putting my gear on, listen to the team-talk, pull my jersey on and run out.'

Instead of the walkabout, he remained at Crystal Palace 'playing cards [and] doing what rugby players do when they are waiting for the weekend.' Syd Hynes went with some of the Leeds players to Lingfield Park races later in the day and had an arrangement with Eyre to pay a visit to Hynes's sister Brenda in the evening, as she lived not far from where they were staying. Brenda, at one point Miss Great Britain Health and Strength, was married to a former Mr. Universe by the name of Len Sell who ran two body-building gyms in London. Eyre says 'Sid and Len had arranged that we would go round. Obviously I knew Brenda from Bewerley Street School. She didn't know we were coming and, when we walked in on the

Friday evening, there were shrieks.' Leeds and London seemed a lot further apart in those days and the opportunities to see family in the south would have been rare.

Trinity's Geoff Oakes remembers one particular incident during the eve of the final. 'The night before the match, Trailly gave us a couple of hours off. We all zoomed into London somewhere. Anyway, we were a little bit late. I think we had to be back at half-past ten, something like that. We told the taxi driver that we were going to be in big trouble if we're late. 'Leave it to me', he said. So we pulled up outside Baileys and Trailly's sat in a wicker chair on a balcony at the entrance. The taxi driver got out and said 'My fault governor, had a puncture.' Trailly replied, 'Don't give me that bollocks, else I'll chin you!' That became a bit of a saying among the players. Ray Owen was always saying it.'

The wives and girlfriends of the Leeds players were due to set off from Headingley by coach to catch the 7.45a.m. London train from Leeds station on the Saturday morning and Kath Crosby, the wife of the Leeds hooker, has a particular memory of some of their arrangements on the eve of the final. 'A lot of us slept at Mick Clark's, three to a bed, there were eight of us. I was from York and the bus went from Leeds early so a lot of us who were 'out of towners' stayed there. It was very kind of them to ask us.' She reflects on contemporary expectations of 'WAGS' compared to their experiences in 1968. 'Nowadays, you'd go down early and stop at a hotel. But, you know, you wouldn't swap those experiences.'

For the supporters, actually getting a ticket for the final was no easy task as there was tremendous demand from fans of both sides and neutrals, to watch what looked like being an evenly matched game between the season's two most successful and entertaining clubs. One person who experienced particular difficulties was the 55 year old licensee of the Queen's Head Hotel, Ferry Fryston near Castleford, Billy Stott. He was the man who kicked the long distance last minute penalty that won Trinity the Challenge Cup in 1946, a display that won him the inaugural Lance Todd Trophy. But his celebrity status appears to have cut no ice 22 years later and he had become resigned to watching the match on television. He told the *Yorkshire Evening Post*, 'I wanted to go to Wembley with three friends but up to the weekend [before the match] I hadn't got a ticket. Eventually, I managed to get hold of one but only after we'd done a fair amount of running about in the car.'

The stories that are told of what has happened on trips to and from Wembley frequently outlast memories of the match itself. Nevertheless, at a time when London seemed a much more distant place than it does now, the experiences of those travelling to Wembley for that 1968 Challenge Cup final are worthy of note and, for many, it was their first experience of the Metropolis.

Bearing in mind that 1968 was the fourth occasion during the sixties that Trinity had reached Wembley, it was not surprising that in 1975 an ITV comedy series on the adventures of folk travelling to a rugby league cup final was commissioned. It was written by Alan Plater and, based on Chaucer's *Canterbury Tales*, was entitled *Trinity Tales*. Starring Bill Maynard, of *Selwyn Foggitt* and *Heartbeat* fame, as 'Stan the fryer', the programmes institutionalised the important process of 'getting there' for a group of supporters going down in a mini-bus.

'How are you getting there?' after 'have you got your ticket?' were the most asked questions of fans once semi-final victory had been clinched and there were plenty of options. Wakefield Trinity Supporters' Club were, for example, some three weeks before the final, taking bookings for their day train excursion. 'Depart Sat. 11th May approx. 8.00 a.m. from Westgate. Return from Kings Cross app. 11.45 p.m. Fare 52/-,' detailed a piece in Trinity's programme for the Championship quarter-final against Castleford. By the time of that mid-week match, on the evening of 24th April, only five vacancies were left on their weekend trip, leaving the Trinity Social Club (which was to become the famous Wakefield Theatre Club and then a bowling alley) at 10.00 a.m. on the day before the game, at an inclusive cost of £10.

The gang I knocked about with planned - *Trinity Tales* style - to hire a self-drive mini-bus to get us to and from the match but the arrangement didn't work out quite as straightforwardly as we'd hoped. We were required to sort out our own insurance for the vehicle but it proved rather more difficult than we had anticipated because of the youth and inexperience of those who were set to drive. Most of us were still in our teens but eventually we found a company prepared to offer cover to drivers below the age of 21 and everything was in place for our trip. Unfortunately, only two days before we were due at leave, the company folded and our plans fell apart. We hurriedly snapped up tickets for a train from Wakefield which departed very late on the Friday evening.

I am reliant on the memories of Bob Harrison, one of the gang I travelled with, for some of the detail of that weekend. At the time I worked with him at the Yorkshire Electricity Board's offices on Denby Dale Road, Wakefield, where the Sainsbury's supermarket is now located. As well as working together, we both went on to play amateur rugby league for the same side and were part of a large group of lads who went drinking in the centre of Wakefield most Friday and Saturday evenings. Harrison's recollection of the Friday evening before the game is that around a dozen of us caught the midnight special from Wakefield's Kirkgate station after we had completed a pub crawl which had taken us from the Chancery, in Wood Street, to the Wakefield Arms, next to the station.

Another member of our drinking gang at the time was Mick Slater, a gas board engineer from Flanshaw, and he has a particular recollection of what happened as we entered one pub as we made our way down Kirkgate. Like a lot of young fans at the time we had a range of Trinity-related songs which became louder and more frequent as the beer took effect. One of the them, at a time of increasing racial sensitivities, was, 'When The Whites Go Marching In'. Slater says 'Every match we used to sing it. It was nothing untoward but I'm sure that either at the Harewood Arms or the Grey Horse somebody said, 'Ay up. You don't want to be singing that. There's a few coloured lads in t'back.' It could have caused a bit of problem but Wakefield Trinity played in white.'

Unless you've had the experience, it's very difficult to describe the feeling of being part of a massive throng from the same city on a sporting pilgrimage to Wembley. To this day, I take great pleasure in the wit, banter and general friendliness of a rugby league crowd - from whatever club - on its way to and from this great occasion. In Wakefield late that night, as the pubs were closing, the air had a beery bonhomie and a feeling of overwhelming common purpose. The station was awash with red, white and blue. There were scarves, bobble-hats, rosettes, in those days very many of them, like mine, home made. There were banners and our gang's - with 'Wakefield Trinity' in massive letters - was one of the biggest on parade. It was to proudly head a fans' march down Pall Mall the following morning but sadly end the day abandoned in the gents' toilet of a Soho pub.

Bob Harrison recalls, 'The platform at Kirkgate was

packed with loads of supporters all singing the Wakefield song. It went, 'Hello, hello. We are the Wakefield boys. We're gonna win the Challenge Cup. We're gonna win the League. We will follow the Champions.' I can remember someone letting off stink bombs.' Mick Slater recollects another song during that cup run which featured each of the players in the Trinity team. It went to the tune of 'Nick Nack Paddywack..' and started 'Number One. He can run, used to play for Featherstone. Nick Nack Paddywack, give the boy a hand. We're the best team in the land.'

The twelve of us squashed into one of the old style individual passenger compartments with seats for eight facing each other and a sliding door leading to a corridor to other compartments and the toilet. These old compartments had luggage racks above the seats with a kind of criss-cross thin rope material and, for the not too discerning, it doubled as a hammock-type arrangement where it was possible to stretch out. Harrison says that he and I climbed up to try and get some sleep amid a frankly impossible environment of continuing alcohol consumption and excited banter.

One of us, however, had to forego our comfort as the journey proceeded. We discovered that one of our number was - unbeknown to any of us - an epileptic and he proceeded to have a fit as we travelled. Mick Slater describes the response of his companions. 'He had a bit of a shaking fit and we, wanting our kip, put him up on the luggage rack. There was a bit of netting above the pictures so we bobbed him in there and he slept very nicely. I think he woke up just short of London.'

The journey took considerably longer than the modern two hour dash but we passed the time with occasional attempts at sleep, card games, chatter about the day ahead, and team selection for the match, particularly in the light of Neil Fox's enforced absence through injury. Wakefield Trinity weren't by any means a one-man team at that time but the absence of a player of his calibre - with considerable big match experience and the ability to turn a game - was a massive blow to us. And, for those of us who had grown up hero-worshipping Foxy from being young kids, there would be something significant missing from this important match. His injury had taken some of the shine off the occasion.

Our train got us into London not long after dawn on the day of the final. Slater recalls, 'We got into Kings Cross, I think it must have been five or six o'clock in the morning. I think we'd seen the sights of London - we'd seen it all, even Buckingham Palace- by about 7.30 a.m. We went back to Trafalgar Square and into the Lyons Corner House and we all had a coffee. Ian Taylor, he'd taken his toothbrush with him and he went down a little stairway to some toilets and he was brushing away. But he hadn't taken any toothpaste.'

Eric Timmins, who served on the board at Wakefield until quite recently, went to the final with his friends Eric 'Pud' Hemingway, and Barry and Keith Lodge, who were cousins. Their routine was similar to many Trinity supporters, with several pints in Wakefield pubs before they boarded a midnight 'special' train from Kirkgate station to Kings Cross. They were aware of the Covent Garden pubs opening at the crack of dawn but found themselves being questioned about where in the fruit and vegetable market they worked. Unable to blag their way round the question, they were turned away on the basis that the establishments were only open for those working there.

Timmins says his gang then took the tube to Hyde Park, arriving there around 6.30 a.m. 'When we got to the park lake and saw all the unattended boats, we couldn't resist a row, having seen other Trinity fans doing the same. But we all made a swift return to the shore and a quick exit on the sudden appearance of a park ranger.' Bob Harrison remembers that among the London sights our group visited that morning was No. 10 Downing Street. 'I think, by 11 a.m. we were running out of places to visit. By this time, Leicester Square was opening up and we started another pub crawl. One pub had a cowboy and Indian type theme. After the match, that's where we left the banner.'

Those who travelled by road, coming down from the Yorkshire area at least, invariably used the A1. The M1, now the main tributary, was at that point only partially constructed and the A1 was a very different animal to nowadays where it is motorway in places and mostly dual carriageway elsewhere.

Robert Smith was 14 years old at the time and, although nowadays a resident of Wakefield, he originates from Leeds and supports the Loiners. He travelled to the match by car with the family of his friend who lived next door to him. 'I came home from school on the Friday and was sent to bed early as we left Leeds at 11.30 p.m. to travel down by car. We were all very excited and, therefore, didn't get much sleep on the way down. I remember the sun rising before we got to London and that was the first time I can ever recall seeing such a wonderful sight.'

Martyn Sadler, nowadays managing editor of the *Rugby Leaguer and League Express* newspaper, fervently followed Trinity and was in his late teens at the time of the final. He travelled down the A1 with his parents and his brother and girlfriend, crammed into the family's Volkswagen Beetle, setting off from Wakefield at 5.00 a.m. on the Saturday. The car had an unfortunate habit of backfiring when idling, sending passers-by scuttling for cover. While Sadler had previously been to London when Trinity won the Cup in 1963, it was his mother's first ever trip down south, despite the fact that she was by then in her late forties. 'I'm not sure what she was expecting, but as we travelled down, getting nearer to London, she kept commenting that the houses in the south of England didn't in fact look much different to those in Wakefield and that southerners didn't necessarily look richer than those of us from the north.'

Sadler recalls that perhaps the most notable memory of that day for his mother was not what was to unfold later at Wembley stadium but what happened as they were walking down Oxford Street before the match. 'It was the height of the 'swinging sixties' and although my mother had never really been a pop music fan, she was suddenly transfixed by the sight of Cliff Richard walking towards us on the pavement. Cliff, who was at the height of his fame, was good looking, smart and quite charismatic. He smiled briefly at my mother as he walked past and she then stood and watched him as he disappeared into the distance. She wouldn't move until he had totally disappeared from view. That was the moment when she thought that London really was a special place and when she became a Cliff Richard fan for life.'

The Sadler family may have been pretty uncomfortable in an overcrowded Beetle but, for others travelling down the A1 that day, their situation would have seemed the height of luxury. Roger Ingham, whose unique commentaries on the fell-racing at Kilnsey and sheep-shearing at the Great Yorkshire Show I have enjoyed for years, tells of the experience of three of his Skipton pals; Noel Stuttard, Paul Stamforth and Steve Smith. They had been playing in a County Cup U18s soccer final at Guiseley on the Friday evening. Ingham, who was going to London by train the following morning, was at the rain-soaked soccer match and took the lads' football gear back to Skipton so that they could head off south straight afterwards.

'They set off to hitch-hike,' he recalls. 'They were like drowned rats on the football field to start with. Then they muddled their way over to the A1, hitch-hiked down there and finished up getting a lift in the back of a coal wagon and it lashed it down on them all the way. They landed in London in the early hours. I've hitch-hiked in the back of wagons, you soon get frozen with the breeze fairly blowing up with the lashing rain.' According to Ingham, Smith ended up with pneumonia as a result of the expedition.

One individual who travelled to Wembley in a little more comfort came from a good deal further. On the day before the final, the *Yorkshire Evening Post* reported that Hank Stram, the coach of the Kansas City Chiefs American Football team, was heading to the game in search of kickers who might be suitable for his sport and willing to head across the Atlantic. The paper's readers were given an insight into American Football and told that teams like the Chiefs would, '...have the support of massed bands of girls in stylish uniforms, cheer leaders, mascots and other diversions.' Who would have thought at the time that, almost four and a half decades later, rugby league supporters at Belle Vue and Headingley would also find themselves having to peer around the likes of Daddy Cool, Ronnie the Rhino and hordes of gyrating adolescents in order to see the action?

The article also explained the specific role of a kicker in American Football and said that Stram was arriving in London on the day, '...and hopes to reach Wembley in time to see the match which could include some of the game's greatest kickers.' Indeed, Stram did make it to the match and was subsequently reported as being, 'amazed' at what he had seen. 'I was staggered at the sustained attack and ruggedness and amazed that none of the players wore pads,' he was reported as saying.

They Walked on Water

Some youngsters, there to support Leeds, were part of a hundred strong schoolboy party organised by volunteer teachers and supported by the local evening newspaper. Many of the boys were on their first ever visit to the capital and entered a 'Report the Day' competition run by the paper and some of their recollections were printed in it during the following week. Philip Close, a pupil at Cow Close County Secondary School in Farnley was one of a number who seemed a little underwhelmed by parts of the trip. He wrote, 'From the Tower we went on a tour of 'swinging London', but I didn't see anything to confirm this.' John Bevan, from Woodhouse County Secondary School was unimpressed by the Prime Minister's residence. 'With Harold Wilson being in a high position you would expect to find him in a mansion house or villa - well, a large house.' He suggested tacking a house for the Prime Minister on to the end of the Palace of Westminster.

There were the usual expressions of surprise at southern prices for items on sale, particularly near to the stadium. A lad by the name of A. Charlton, from Belle Isle County Secondary School noted, 'There were scores of men trying to sell souvenir photographs, rosettes and miniature cups. The prices of these things were atrocious but people still flocked to buy them.' But Stephen Lucciarini, of St. Joseph's School, clearly wasn't put off by the cost of the foot-long hot dogs he'd probably never come across before. 'I got three and two cans of pop,' he wrote.

Interestingly, none of the contributions published made any mention of what those youngsters thought of being present at a match which could hardly have been richer in drama and controversy.

Chapter Seven

And the heavens opened

The odd thing about it is that some of the worst weather conditions I have ever experienced during a rugby league match, and certainly the worst for any Challenge Cup final at Wembley, go almost unremarked in the National Meteorological records for 11 May, 1968. Their Air Ministry Diary for the weather at Kew that day notes, 'Fine early becoming mainly cloudy with sunny intervals. Frequent showers in afternoon with thunder at times. Rather cool with winds S.W to Wly. Light to Moderate.' The rainfall total for Kew that day, 'was 3mm, but 1.2mm of this fell in a 20-min period between 1300 and 1400 GMT' and, according to the Meteorological Office, 'this is still only moderate-heavy rainfall.' The records of 'significant rainfall' for May, 1968 contain no mention of the day of the final.

The television archive, news reports and photographs of the day prove that none of us imagined what Robert Gate describes as, 'freak monsoon conditions.' Tony Hannan in his biography *Being Eddie Waring* notes that, 'As the dark skies opened high above Wembley's old twin towers, producing freak conditions more suited to water polo than rugby, no-one had ever seen anything like it.' But because Kew is over five miles to the south, it is quite conceivable that the 20 minute period of rain noted there between 1300 and 1400 GMT that day was the edge of the memorable storm which hit Wembley a little later, carried by those light to moderate south west to westerly winds.

Having been wandering round London from the early hours, my gang - few of whom had been to Wembley before - arrived quite early at the stadium before the weather had deteriorated. Mick Slater says, 'When we got there it was beautiful. It was red hot.' There was a keen sense of anticipation as we climbed the steps to our terrace position. This may have been the venue of England's soccer World Cup success in 1966 but, more importantly to most of us, it was where Neil Fox had scored that magnificent length of the field try against Hull in 1960, kicked those crucial drop-goals against Huddersfield in 1962 and where Harold Poynton got that great interception against Wigan the following year.

We had the cheapest tickets, behind the dressing-room end goal posts to the Royal Box side of the pitch and, in those days there were no seats at each end. As we emerged from the passage at the top of the steps near our position, I remember being struck, firstly, by how big the inside of the stadium was at first sight and, secondly, how gloomy it now looked as the clouds were gathering on what had previously been a bright and sunny May day. My first real childhood memory of Wembley had been watching Trinity's appearance there in 1960 on the television when they played Hull in bright sunlight and I had, from that time, somehow associated the nation's biggest sporting stage with bright, cheerful weather, not the increasing darkness. And with the gloom came the rain. 'There was a deluge,' remembers Mick Slater, 'and we always said that if that had been at Odsal or Headingley it would have been called off.'

Then, as now, some fans gambled on picking tickets up at the venue on the day. Rugby league novelist Geoff Lee was working in London at the time and picked one up from a Castleford fan with a spare one belonging to his father who had died the previous week. However, on going to his seat, he found a woman sitting in it and was told by her - almost gleefully - that his ticket was a forgery. A Wembley steward became involved in the dispute and told Lee and a few other disgruntled fans to go to an office right at the top of the stadium. There he joined around thirty other fans who were all informed that their tickets had been stolen from a club in Kippax and were no longer valid.

Fortunately, because they had bought them in good faith, the stadium authorities allowed them all to stand on the terracing behind the posts. Geoff Lee makes the point that he had paid 17/6d for his ticket and finished up with those - like my mates and I - who had only paid 5/-. But the consolation was that at least we were dry.

Eric Timmins and his pals had gone round the London sights during the morning seeing many hundreds of Wakefield and Leeds fans who were doing the same. They headed for Wembley for lunchtime drinks before the match. Timmins recalls, 'Sat inside the pub, the Centurian possibly, talking rugby and consuming several pints of poor London beer, we had no idea of the change in the weather. I got split up from the other lads and remember stepping out of the front door as the heavens opened again, putting my coat over my head and walking to the ground. By the time I arrived I was absolutely drenched from head to toe.'

The weather had serious consequences as well for

They Walked on Water

Leeds supporter Mel Reuben. 'I had just got engaged a few weeks before the final. My fiancée bought me a brown suede jacket as an engagement present. I decided to wear it for my trip to London. After leaving Wembley Central railway station I walked down to the famous Greyhound pub. Just as I was waiting to cross the road, the heavens opened and I got thoroughly soaked. As I tried to dry off in the pub I took my jacket off, then everyone in the pub started to laugh. I suddenly noticed that my once clean white shirt was covered with huge brown stains!'

Harry Jepson, at the time Hunslet's Secretary and now President of the Leeds club, remembers his cup final routine at the time and his experience, with his wife, Mary, of the weather that day. 'During previous visits to Wembley I got involved with a couple of people who always had lunch at the Conservative Club at Wembley which was next to the Hilton Hotel. On the site now - believe it or not - is Mahatma Ghandi House, the Conservative Club has disappeared. There were about 30 or 40 people there, it was a nice little place. Kick off time came nearer and we decided to walk down to Wembley and when we got almost to the stadium, a few drops of rain started. Mary and I hadn't a coat so I said, 'Come on, we'll shelter under this tree - it's only a shower.' Well, what a shower it was! And we had to walk right round the ground so we were wet through by the time we got to our seats on the far side.'

Roger Ingham is some way behind Jepson's record of sixty-seven attendances at rugby league cup finals but can still boast of being at almost every one since 1959. He is also quite unique in claiming that he actually owes his life to the occasion. His father, a Keighley supporter, was in London for his team's appearance in the 1937 final and met his mother, who came from Gargrave, and was on her first ever trip to the capital to see the decorations for the Coronation of King George VI which was taking place the following week.

Ingham has a unique way of describing his subsequent arrival in the world. 'In those days they didn't go down - all the teenage lasses - with it all hanging out and flapping up and down and oscillating from side to side. They wore their best frock in those days - did things right - so it was another seven years before I turned up. The most prominent and notable scoring achievement in my life was when Lew Bevan ran 40 yards in the Challenge Cup semi-final replay against Wakefield and sent Keighley to Wembley. Otherwise I wouldn't have been here, nor my brother either.'

For someone who has attended nearly fifty finals, it is testimony to the conditions on that day in May 1968, that Roger Ingham has such a clear recollection of what happened when he arrived at the capital. 'When we got off the train in London - we were going to have a walk round the sights - we didn't get far when it came on hailstones, lightning, thunder - and so you could imagine Wembley fairly copping it. So we finished up taking refuge in a pub, then we made a dash to the station. I had a bit of wisdom at that juncture. I bought a newspaper. I thought it'll keep me dry on the way up from Wembley Park station.'

'We got there and it was absolutely monsooning down. We couldn't get off the train hardly because there were that many taking refuge on the platform. It was full upstairs and down at Wembley Park station. There were hailstones, lightning and thunder again. So I put the newspaper over my head. It did relent a bit walking up Wembley Way, just a little bit.' As he entered the stadium, there was another downpour as Ingham and his friends endeavoured to find the seats which had been obtained for them by Trinity's David Jeanes, a lifelong friend, also from the Skipton area. He describes the impact of the weather conditions on those spectators who were seated near to the pitch and not undercover. 'Those in the front seats and the first twenty rows were all coming back. It was jammed in the concourse then it slowed a bit. We got to the seats and there were guys with shirts off, wringing them out! That was the prelude to what it was like.'

Ken Rollin's wife, Anne, had travelled with the Leeds wives and girlfriends by train that morning, checking in and lunching at the Park Lane Hotel in London, where the Leeds party would spend the Saturday night. 'When we arrived at Wembley, we had to sit in the bus for over an hour before we could get out, to walk from where it was parked. It was raining so heavily and, of course, we were all dolled up.' Tony Crosby's wife, Kath, says, 'There were bursts of rain interspersed with really hot sun. The sun dried it up quickly. And of course we'd got our best gear on which you had to look after. We were all in our blue and gold - all dressed up - and we just didn't want to get wet. So we had to scurry in between the showers to get into Wembley.'

Trinity's Ian Brooke says that on the morning of the final no-one had really thought about the weather. 'In those days the grounds you played on weren't anywhere near the standards of Wembley. It was just like a carpet and you thought - with the ground staff and everything - a little bit of rain would sort of just disperse, or they'd have the staff there to get rid of it. It was the national stadium, so you were expecting those things to be done.'

But it was not just a little bit of rain. When the Trinity players had been to look at the pitch, before their dressing room preparations, the weather had been fine with bright sunshine and Brooke describes how they were blissfully unaware of how bad the conditions had become. 'We were all in the dressing room doing everything that you usually do - rub-down, get your strapping, getting your kit on - and someone came in and said, 'God, there's been a hell of a thunderstorm.There's bloody puddles all over the pitch.' Brooke reckoned they got word of the weather perhaps half-an-hour before kick-off. 'So really, nobody realised, and we hadn't had a look because we weren't in a position to go outside.'

For Leeds custodian Bev Risman, 'We weren't panicking, you don't even think about the match being called off or anything like that, but when we saw the rain on our way to the ground it was absolutely horrendous. My mind was in an absolute tizzy and I think everybody else's was because it was totally unexpected really. I don't think really anybody realised until you got out onto the pitch that the conditions were so bad.'

Barry Seabourne says 'When we arrived there it was sunny. We all went out to get a feel of the place and were talking to the Leeds schoolchildren who were sitting on the side where the dog track was. Then we went in to get changed and somebody burst in and shouted, 'The pitch is flooded!' We couldn't believe it. It was bouncing down with rain.'

Norman Hazell, a prominent Wakefield councillor over many years and a former Mayor, travelled to Wembley in a party of around 16 friends and relatives in a convoy of three cars. He was driven by Peter Fox, Don and Neil's older brother, who he had known over many years and worked with at Yorkshire Copperworks in Leeds. 'I'll never forget, we parked in an Oxfam shop's car park and they were charging five shillings per car,' a significant amount in those days, even if it was for a good cause.

'When we got into the ground, I was sitting next to Peter near the centre-line facing the Royal Box. We were horrified when we saw the ground because there was water standing everywhere. It was a terrible situation. When the wind changed and started blowing in our faces, the rain came tippling down on top of us. We were near the front almost in the first or second row and we jumped up and ran back up the gangways - so many other people did - and yet amazingly the game went on. If it had been a normal match, I think it would have been impossible. It was ludicrous.'

The occasion has gone down in sporting history as the 'Watersplash final'. Credit for first use of the term would appear to go to *Yorkshire Evening Post* reporter Arthur Haddock. His story appeared on the front and back pages of the *Sports Echo* edition of the paper during the evening, with headlines referring to '...watersplash Wembley.' The downpours, according to Haddock, '...soaked fans on their way down Olympic Way, temporarily drove the band of the Coldstream Guards to cover, and brought out 21 men to fork the sodden turf.'

Other reporters there that day also waxed lyrical on the state of the pitch. The *Guardian*'s Harold Mather noted that at one point, '...there was so much water on the pitch that it was considerably more suitable to some form of aquatic sport than for football.' Indeed, Gavin Gray in the *Sunday Telegraph* suggested that the match had, '...been played in conditions more suitable for water polo...' Under a photograph of action from the game referring to 'surfing', the *Morning Star*'s Stanley Levenson dubbed it, '...the great Wembley water show...' Alan Thomas in the *Daily Express* wrote that, 'The drains could not cope with the pre-match downpour and before the kick-off there were 20 men on the pitch with forks trying to release huge pools of water. They failed...the sodden, spongy surface....became miniature lakes as the rain came down like stair-rods before half-time.'

Daily Telegraph correspondent Bob Pemberton asserted that, 'No final at Wembley has been played under such atrocious conditions,' while under the headline, 'Dramatic final that should not have been played,' the *Huddersfield Daily Examiner*'s scribe, The Scout, opined, 'Had there been any of the pushing down of the head of the tackled player, as is so often seen in games, someone must surely have been drowned.'

The *Sunday Mirror*'s report the following day reassured the soccer fans among its readers with a stark headline above a photograph of players splashing around during the match that, 'THIS WILL NOT AFFECT THE FA CUP FINAL.' The West Bromwich Albion and Everton clash was scheduled for the following Saturday and the paper included a quote from a Wembley spokesman saying, 'The water will be pumped off and it will be in perfect condition again by next Tuesday or Wednesday.'

In his letter of thanks to the Rugby Football League's Secretary-General, Bill Fallowfield for hospitality at the Wembley final, kept in the BBC archive in Caversham, David Attenborough, then BBC 2's Controller, summed it up well. Obviously not entirely familiar with the 13-a-side code he remarked that, '...even I could see that the possibilities of playing really skilful rugby were cramped not to say damped.'

David Lawrenson, in his *Rugby League Miscellany* argues that 'The match should never have been played but with live television coverage on the BBC and thousands of fans making the trip down to London the game was allowed to go on.' Dave Hawley, the Trinity loose-forward that day, recalled in the *Times*'s SportsFile: 'Caught in Time - Leeds win the Challenge Cup, 1968', penned by Greg Stuthers in 2010, that 'If the match had been held anywhere else but Wembley I don't think it would have gone ahead. But because there were

80,000 people in the ground, most of whom had travelled hundreds of miles from the north, we had to go ahead and play.'

As Secretary of Hunslet at the time, Harry Jepson had, on several occasions, been involved in matches where the referee had had to determine whether the pitch was in a fit condition for the game to go ahead. More than most, perhaps, he understood the dilemma facing the man in the middle at the 1968 final. 'I was a bit sorry for the referee, John Hebblethwaite, because the rain started, continued and when we got to our seats, probably three-quarters of an hour before kick-off, there were already pools of water standing on the ground with the ground staff were trying desperately to get rid of it. But they hadn't the equipment to clear the volume of water and doubts began to be raised in lots of people's minds that this game won't get played.'

There was considerable speculation as the huge crowd assembled in the stadium whether it might become, at the very last minute, the first rugby league final at Wembley to be called off. Jepson's view was that this was very much a likely option. 'We were very, very surprised when the referee decided that the game would go on. But we tried to put ourselves in his position. There were 80,000 people there and it was a momentous decision to have to make. I don't know who was Chairman of the RL at the time but there would have been very serious discussions. There was the 'Cup and Rules Committee' controlling the game in those days and they were all there and would no doubt have been having meetings but they were faced with a very difficult position. They didn't know how long the rain was going to last. They didn't know what the weather was going to be like afterwards. Everybody was looking forward to the game, especially the two teams.'

Jepson continues, 'When the teams came out from the dressing rooms which were down to our right they paddled to the centre line and had the pre-match preliminaries - introduction of the teams - even though the rain was coming down in sheets. Everybody around me was thinking what are we going to see today?'

Despite the weather the customary menu of pre-match entertainment went ahead as usual. From 1.30 p.m. to 2.20 p.m. the assembling crowd was entertained by a programme of music performed by the Band of the Grenadier Guards. As spectators entered the stadium they were handed a printed song-sheet for the *Daily Express* Community Singing between 2.20 p.m. and 2.50 p.m. The songs listed were, 'Fall In and Follow Me', 'Congratulations', 'When The Saints Go Marching In', 'The Last Waltz', 'Puppet On A String', 'John Brown's Body', 'On Ilkely Moor Baht 'At', 'My Girl's A Yorkshire Girl', 'Bye Bye Blackbird', 'Tears' and the Leeds team's anthem 'The End Of The Road'. Bill Scott-Coomber conducted the Community Singing and he was accompanied by the Band of the Coldstream Guards who were to get soaked before the match and even wetter when they reappeared at half-time.

Aside from struggling with the weather, there were other traumas confronting the predominantly Yorkshire crowd that day. Peter Astbury and other non-playing members of the Leeds squad were seated at the side of the Royal Box where tickets cost £2 each, a huge amount then. 'I remember David Hick getting seven bottles of beer in plastic cups. Twenty-one shillings he paid. He was one of the young boys in the squad. We poured our beer in the cups and his had a hole in the bottom! He said 'I've just paid twenty-one shillings and I can't get a drink."

Chapter Eight

Inside, where it was dry

The Rugby Football League's archives, held by the University of Huddersfield, offer a fascinating insight into the careful preparation that goes into the game's big occasions. I have had the privilege of being a guest at them over the years and had, perhaps, never understood the complexities of preparing for the smooth running of a major event until studying the files relating to what was went on both on the pitch and behind the scenes at Wembley in 1968.

Since the rebuilding of the national stadium and the return of the showpiece occasion there in 2007, guests of the RFL have been wined and dined in offshoot areas such as the Great Hall for the bulk and the Atrium. Prior to that, in the old Twin Towers, everyone was accommodated in one large dining area. The Luncheon arrangement in 1968 included a lengthy top table off which eight separate tables were placed at right-angles. Three of these catered specifically for Rugby League Council and Life Members with the rest for a variety of attendees from a range of different backgrounds.

It is particularly interesting to note that, while nowadays the RFL rarely attract royalty to Challenge Cup finals and often settle for relatively minor politicians as their chief guest, in 1968, not only was the Duke of Kent present but, seated at the centre of the top table, was the then Prime Minister, Harold Wilson. Looking back at the political pressure he was under at that particular time, Wilson could have been forgiven for giving the match a miss. Across the Channel, our closest neighbour France was experiencing student riots and a very unstable environment but Wilson's immediate concerns would have been on the domestic front.

His Labour Government was deeply unpopular at the time and was facing considerable resistance from trade unions over wage restraint. There was the strong prospect of a rebellion by Wilson's own backbenchers the following week when a new Prices and Incomes Bill, promising further restrictions, was due for its second reading. The Conservative Party had made massive gains in the local elections which had been held two days earlier and the headline in the *Yorkshire Evening Post* the day before the final - 'Wilson Faces A Leadership Crisis' - typified what much of the press were saying that weekend.

Seated alongside Wilson were the President of the RFL, the Earl of Derby and John Spencer Wills, who was Chairman of Wembley. Facing them on tables four and five respectively, the guests included David Attenborough - the Controller of BBC2 - and Peter Dimmock, a well-known BBC sports presenter. Some way along the top table from the Prime Minister was Denis Howell MP, a former soccer referee who gave distinguished service as Sports Minister and proved to be a good friend to rugby league during my early days in the Commons.

Other than Arthur Lewis, a Londoner and the MP for

West Ham North since 1950, the only other MPs who appear to have been present that day were my predecessor as MP for Wakefield, Walter Harrison, and the Leeds MP, Merlyn Rees, who attended with his two sons. There were far more there from the Lords than the Commons but what is more striking - and perhaps reflected the background of Bill Fallowfield, then Secretary of the RFL - is the extent of the representation of those with an obvious armed forces, and particularly RAF, background. At the time Fallowfield had been appointed to the League in 1946, he had been a Flight Lieutenant in the RAF, stationed at Finningley, near Doncaster. At least ten of the guests were of high military rank at a time when the playing of rugby league was another quarter of a century away from being permitted.

One gentleman with a particularly distinguished military background had tendered his apologies. Field-Marshall Montgomery of Alamein declined, probably because of increasing frailty. But while he was unable to be there in person, he made it absolutely clear which team would have his support. 'Monty' had presented Trinity with the Cup after their victory over Wigan in 1963 and he had subsequently become an Honorary Patron of the club. Before the 1968 final he had written to the Trinity players 'ordering them' to win it.

Guests at the Wembley Luncheon also included some notable names from other sports. Herbert Sutcliffe, the renowned Yorkshire cricketer was present, as was Walter Winterbottom, a leading figure in soccer and on the Sports Council at the time. Sir Stanley Rous, a key figure in the 1966 World Cup success, appears to have been a late withdrawal from the guest list, and, perhaps reflecting the quality of relationships between the two codes of rugby at the time, the RFL's notes of who was and who was not attending contained a very definite 'no' alongside the name of R. E. Prescott, Secretary of the Rugby Football Union.

Down at pitch level the Programme of Arrangements for the match set out with military precision the detail of exactly what was to happen. Leeds were to use the North (No.1) dressing room while Wakefield Trinity were allocated the South (No. 2). A lengthy paragraph set out the detail on the subject of the teams entering the arena. The players and officials were to be ready by 2.45 p.m. with the referee responsible for ensuring prompt attention to timing. At exactly 2.48 p.m. the teams were required to line up in numerical order behind the two captains and, 'On receipt of a signal from a member of the Wembley staff standing at the entrance to the arena, the Chairmen of the two clubs shall lead their two teams into the arena, Leeds having Wakefield Trinity on their left.'

Officials were detailed to follow the teams and the programme set out how all concerned should line up, 'to positions between the band and the touchline facing each other approximately ten yards apart on either side of the opening to the Royal Tunnel. When the teams are in position the Chairman and Captain of the Wakefield Trinity team will move to the other end of their line….The Referee and Touch Judges will line up with the Wakefield Trinity team and the Leader of the Community Singing will stand beside the end Touch Judge…' The final paragraph offers a marked contrast to the modern game where jerseys are adorned with sponsors' logos. 'Players shall not wear clothing displaying advertising matter', it stated.

Details of who should sit on the touch-line benches were set out, 'only four persons from each club including the managers and masseurs' and the reserve referee was also seated there, dressed in kit in case he need to take charge of the game.

They Walked on Water

A total of nine paragraphs of the Programme of Arrangements dealt with the Reception of The Duke and Duchess of Kent and Presentation of Teams. The Royal couple did not attend the pre-match banquet but were to be in the Royal Tunnel by no later than 2.48 p.m. to be met by an RFL delegation; its President, the Earl of Derby, Chairman Mr. J. N. Smallwood and Secretary Bill Fallowfield. They were to be accompanied by the Chairman of Wembley Stadium Ltd, Mr. J. Spencer Wills.

This final, then as now, was organised with military precision by the Rugby Football League as the code's showpiece event of the year. But some things cannot be planned for and despite the very best efforts of those organising the occasion factors way beyond their control that day meant that this match very nearly didn't go ahead.

Chapter Nine

And in the dressing rooms

There was perhaps a very gradual dawning among those about to perform on the field that the weather was making the playing conditions somewhat less than ideal. Inevitably, other preoccupations were uppermost as the players from both sides assembled in the dressing rooms and gathered their thoughts before the match began.

John Atkinson was among the Leeds players who went out onto the pitch some time before changing for the match. 'I just thought, oh dear me. Everything I ever wanted in my life from being a little boy has just come true. You look around the ground and there wasn't a space. It was absolutely chocca but we were thinking, it's a bit wet.' It was to get wetter still, even before the kick-off. Back in the dressing room, Atkinson particularly remembers his emotions. 'We were getting ready - sat round - and Roy Francis came and gave each one of us our shirt. I filled up with tears when he gave me mine.'

Syd Hynes recalls that the Leeds team coach had

arrived at the stadium at around 1.30 p.m. 'We walked up the tunnel and had a look at the pitch. The lads were getting a feel of it and then it was back in the dressing room before 2.00. Some of them used to get changed early. I'd get changed about twenty minutes before kick-off. I'd have a couple of cigs and one at half-time, maybe. I was laid back. Other players used to get uptight. Players like that, when you see them up close, really get nervous. But it didn't bother me.'

After going with the players into the Leeds dressing room, Ken Rollin was among those who returned to the pitch. 'I thought my goodness. This isn't good at all. You tend to think, oh, it'll drain fairly well, but it didn't actually.' As someone with detailed knowledge of both the participating teams, Rollin had agreed to act as an advisor to the commentator for the American Sport TV channel who were broadcasting the match live that day. He left the dressing room some time before kick-off to head up high into the stand to the commentary position.

Bev Risman recalls that there was no speculation in the dressing room before the match that it might not go ahead. 'There was nobody coming in saying otherwise, it was just presumed that the match was on and the only person who had that worry was Mr. Hebblethwaite. Once they'd opened the gates and let people through it had to be played.' Leeds second rower, Albert Eyre, adds 'Nobody came in and said, "Oh. It's dodgy." I can't remember anything like that.' Alan Smith remembers that the players could hear the rain and hailstones coming down in the dressing room.

Ian Brooke has no recollection of any debate in the Trinity dressing room around calling the match off. 'I don't know whether Ken [Traill] had, or anybody else but we hadn't had any feedback into the dressing room. As far as we were concerned, it was going ahead.' David Jeanes says he wasn't really aware of how bad things had become outside until water actually started coming into the changing room. 'We all started to think, what on earth's going on here? This is Wembley stadium - our premier stadium - and there was water coming from somewhere into the actual changing room! I can't remember anyone saying before the game that there was a chance it might not take place but it became obvious during the game that it shouldn't have been played. The fact is that everybody said afterwards that it had only been played because it was on television and was the Cup final. Any other game would have been stopped because it was a farce.'

None of those I have spoken to who were in those dressing rooms that day had any idea at the time of possible mounting concern. The weather before the match was bad enough and no-one was to know that, after the kick-off and particularly around and after half-time, it was going to get considerably worse. The archives of the Rugby Football League appear to offer no record or indication of any debate around whether the game should have been given the go-ahead, but it is evident that vigorous discussion did take place over what should happen.

David Hebblethwaite confirms that, in accordance with the game's rules at the time, the decision to give the go-ahead was down to his father alone. But it is clear that the decision that he did make was not necessarily the one favoured by Rugby Football League officials. 'Bill Fallowfield, came in and said they were discussing cancelling it because it was that bad out there. They were in touch with the groundsman and the he came in and said, "There's nothing to worry about at all because this is the best drainage in the country."' His response would seem to indicate that Wembley stadium had never previously experienced quite what was to happen.

David Hebblethwaite remembers that conditions did improve a little some time before the start of the match. 'It was drying out until it came down again and it was just too much. Fallowfield was the one that wanted to cancel it. My dad's response was, "You'll end up with having a riot on your hands if you do." A lot of lads in those days, they didn't go on holiday. Wembley was their holiday and they'd saved up for it - a pound here, ten shillings there - just for that weekend. Fallowfield turned round and said to my dad, "Look. It's up to you. If you want to play it, we'll play it," and he said, "I don't think I've much option with the crowd out there."'

John Hebblethwaite, according to his son, felt the conditions that day were unprecedented. 'He'd never ever experienced anything like that and I don't think any of the players had either. He always said that there was no way he would stop the game. He would keep it going unless there was serious injury. It was that wet, players weren't even getting dirty.'

Albert Eyre describes the weather that day as, 'something else. We could hear it - the rumbling - and obviously we got reports saying it was going to be wet.' With the knowledge of the conditions there was some discussion of the tactics to be adopted during the match in the Leeds dressing room. Risman describes, 'Roy Francis had psyched us all up in whatever way he usually did beforehand, trying to tell us it was just an ordinary game, nothing to worry about, just get stuck in and what have you. It was obviously going to be a bit wet so he mentioned a good kicking game and to make sure we didn't make any mistakes, that sort of thing to concentrate on our handling.' Albert Eyre concurs, 'Roy just told us to play the game we'd played all year. We did throw the ball about - too much sometimes.'

Barry Seabourne remembers that Francis always left his

players to their own thoughts. 'He believed in letting you do it rather than him say stuff. He'd just go through basic things. If you got your basics right, that was it as far as he was concerned. Everybody was pretty skilful in the side so they all had something to contribute.'

Harold Poynton's recollection from the Wakefield camp is that they were not really aware of just how bad the conditions were and, as a consequence, there was minimal preparation for what was to come. 'Not a thought about it, no discussion on tactics.' Hooker Geoff Oakes, out of the team because of his injury, was also in the dressing room. 'To be honest, tactics weren't discussed that much anyway. It was a lot more playing off the cuff in those days. Lads might have got together in a little group and said "We might do this" but it was totally on the hoof.'

David Jeanes remembers Ken Traill's comments to him before the team went out. 'Ken was, I think, my number one critic in terms of my handling, so obviously he knew that I would be knocking on here, there and everywhere. So it was a matter of, "Make sure you've got plenty of resin on your hands before you get out there and don't let's have you doing the normal cherry-picking." He used to call me The Cherry-Picker. The tactics were just get stuck in and play your normal game.'

Ian Brooke's view is that the Trinity side of that era was good enough to handle most conditions regardless. 'We'd already done the tactics in training and we always felt we were a good enough team to adapt to everything. We had great players in our team, with leaders like Harold Poynton, Neil Fox, we had players - the backbone of the team - that, if it was muddy, if it was dry, whatever the conditions, we were always confident that we could win and we could adjust to it.'

As the players stood in the tunnel waiting to go out, Barry Seabourne says, not surprisingly, that they were all focussing on the game even as they saw the rainwater running in. 'I remember Ray Owen, the Wakefield scrum-half, came over to me - we were stood at the side of one another - and wished me all the best. He said, "Have a good game" and I said the same to him. We were quite good friends - all the players were - as we'd played against each other so many times.'

The reaction when the players emerged from the tunnel to enter the field of play quickly changed, as Ian Brooke vividly remembers. 'When we walked up the slope, that's the first time we all said, "Bloody hell. Look at that!" There were puddles all over.' David Jeanes' thoughts were similar. 'When we finally got out into the tunnel, you're wondering well, what on earth's happening here? You saw these poor old guardsmen wandering about with their bearskins coming down over their eyes because the bloody things were so heavy.'

John Atkinson says that he hadn't particularly noticed the slope of the Wembley tunnel when he had walked out before the game. 'But, when you lined up opposite each other, all you could see was right across to the other end of the ground, just the top of the crowd because of the slope.' He remembers that somebody said "Alright. Come on," and the players started to move towards the pitch. 'We started walking out and it's quiet, then all of a sudden you get this roar. Bernard Watson was in front of me and he stopped. I said, "Come on. It's only the crowd." I had dreamed of playing at Wembley and it had come true.'

Ken Eyre remembers that the sun was out as they entered the field but, like Atkinson, recalls the impact of the crowd on the players. 'The guy in front of you, you could see him - sort of - stumble and you'd think what's up? And then it hits you.' His brother, Albert recalls his coach's instructions to the team for when they entered the field of play. 'I always remember Roy Francis saying to us, "I know you were here yesterday but, when you go out, have a good look round." I was one of those who, if Roy told me to run through a brick wall, I'd do it. So, as we're walking out - you can see it on the video - my head's spinning round. I'd never seen a crowd like it but the weather, well that was something else.'

Not many have the opportunity to take to the field in a Wembley final and, for those who do, their thoughts as they emerge invariably remain with them for the rest of their lives. Alan Smith still vividly does. 'I was as nervous as hell. I look back and it's almost like it came a couple of years too soon. The whole thing was like a dream. You hear stories about coming up the tunnel and how the noise hits you because the crowd can see you first. You can hear the studs, with the players' nervous energy. You walk up and, phew, it's a wonderful experience.' Having found the stadium strangely small when he visited the day before, Smith was struck by how different it seemed as he came out of the tunnel. 'With nearly 100,000 in, it didn't look small. I thought, "What's happened here?" It was incredible, I was in awe and playing against Wakefield, which I didn't want to do, for no other reason than they were still, in my mind, my heroes. I held them in certain respect.'

For Tony Crosby, in his sole Wembley appearance, the emerging moment was never to be forgotten. 'I was pretty overcome with it, really. You just can't describe what it's like coming out there onto that pitch. You don't hear much at all down in the tunnel, but coming out...I wouldn't have minded doing that a few times.'

Almost opposite him, David Jeanes was experiencing similar. 'I'd played just short of thirty games of rugby league. I was on cloud nine because, the week before, I'd played in the Championship final. I'd scored a good try and helped us to win. Just before that I'd had a trial for the Great Britain team and I couldn't believe that I was achieving, in six months, what people who'd been there for years would give their right arm to do, and how lucky I was to be there. Rain or no rain, it was just unbelievable. I remember thinking the old man had put a lot of time into me it felt fantastic, I was kind of paying him back for all he had done.'

Nerves mixed with pride soon took a back seat as the long walk to the centre of the field began. 'All of a sudden the water's on my ankles,' says Ken Eyre. 'Then, I'm thinking, well, that little bit of a side-step I had is going to have to be good here because this is just amazing.' Atkinson describes what he recalls as a film on top of the pitch. 'If it had been at Headingley or Wakefield, it goes through the pitch. You might get a bit of mud but it doesn't lie on the top. I can remember Bernard Watson saying to me, "It's like a swimming pool, this." I replied, "Yes, I know. It's the turf." It was too good, too nice.'

'We didn't know what it was like until we got out onto the ground,' Barry Seabourne notes. 'When we walked onto the pitch there was water over the top of our boots. It was incredible. We'd been out an hour earlier and it was sunshine and firm. We were just staggered as when we went over to meet the royalty. We just stood in water. It was almost comical.' Alan Smith surveyed standing pools as he lined up for the formalities. 'We couldn't tell how deep they were. The grass was so tight, the pitch was so well manicured, it just wouldn't let the water through.'

Albert Eyre has a particular memory of the formal introduction to the Guest of Honour as the teams lined up. 'The Duke of Kent came out. I always remember his face - he'd quite a large nose. They'd put a red mat down for him and, when he stood on it, he just sunk. He pulled a face and I looked down and he was like us, because the water was over his boot tops. He completed his duty but the look on his face was a sight never to be forgotten. They weren't low boot tops then, so it shows how much water was on the pitch. Afterwards we heard rumours that they had to send for some more shoes and socks for him.'

The implications of playing on a soaking, treacherous surface, were apparent even before the match had begun. John Atkinson relates what happened after the players had lined up opposite each other and been introduced to the chief guest. As was traditional, the players were then, one by one, introduced to the crowd. 'The announcer called out, "Number one, Bev Risman", then "number two, Alan Smith." And I heard an "Uh". I looked round and Alan had just fallen straight down. He was the first one to fall - we hadn't even started! He just slipped on the water. Alan said, "No, no. I can't believe I've done this."' In the stand Roger Ingham smiled, 'Alan did tend to do a bit of a bound and a sprint to where he'd be playing on the wing but did a triple somersault.' According to Seabourne, the incident was typical of his team-mate. 'He was really clumsy was Alan. If anything was to happen, it would be Smithy!'

What happened to him right at the start raised serious questions as to whether the go-ahead should have been allowed in the circumstances. *The People*'s reporter, Phil King, was in little doubt as he watched what happened. 'In my opinion Wembley was unfit for rugby. The conditions were well nigh impossible and there was a hint of the spills to come when a Leeds player slipped and turned a complete somersault as he ran from the pre-match presentation to take up his place for the kick-off.'

That moment of introduction to the throng *in situ* and

watching millions by their television sets was something Alan Smith had been looking forward to most. 'As a kid I've watched the finals and I thought the biggest thing was to have your name announced and then you peel off. I'd seen it with Wakefield, "Number one, Gerry Round." Whooah! "Number two, Fred Smith." Whooah! "Number three, Alan Skene." Whooah!... I thought, "It's fantastic is this," to hear my name, it was the proudest day of my life. We went through it all, the National Anthem, my chest was out. And here it comes. I'm listening. The biggest thing I'm looking forward to in my appearance at Wembley, the biggest thing.'

As the players peeled off individually they were passed the ball and Smith relates what happened as he was about to receive it. 'I heard "Number one, Bev Risman." Whooah! It's that loud. Bev goes running away. Then my turn comes and I could hardly hear the call. There was whooah! I turned and just looked for the ball and my feet hit the deepest puddle. I went down and the ball just fell on the floor and I got the biggest cheer of the afternoon. I'm laid there like a turtle. Bev looks at me and says, "You're laid in the puddle!" So the proudest moment of my life turned into the biggest disappointment and embarrassment. It wasn't as though I could get up and say "I hope nobody's seen me."'

Even though the conditions that day were terrible, coming out of the Wembley tunnel was also especially memorable for the referee, John Hebblethwaite. His son David recalls, 'He just said it was the greatest experience of his life with the crowd and everything.' And just as he was unwilling to bow to the pressure there had clearly been to call off the match, Hebblethwaite also indicated to the BBC broadcasting team that he was very much his own man. The main BBC cameras were located on the south side of the Empire stadium, opposite to the Royal Box and, according to

David Hebblethwaite, the broadcasters had asked his father to face the direction of the cameras when supervising the tossing of the coin at the start of the match. But, 'He wouldn't turn his back on the Royal Box. My dad went the other way to the cameras and tossed up facing the Royal Box. He was a very strict person.'

The stresses and pressures of that day were probably only just beginning for John Hebblethwaite at that point but, while the players on both sides were on pretty good money, he was, according to David, officiating for virtually no financial reward at all. 'The choice was £10 or a blazer badge and he took the blazer badge, so he definitely wasn't in it for the money! As an instrument maker, he was on about £12 or £14 a week so the fee was nearly a week's wages.' The recently introduced decimal coin which was used that day at the kick-off. Referee Hebblethwaite's whistle and his blazer badge were on display at the Rugby League Heritage Centre in the George Hotel, Huddersfield, until it's enforced closure in 2013, donated by his family.

Chapter Ten

The first half

While the stadium had been bathed in sunshine as the players came out to start the game, as Ken Eyre relates, the gloom soon returned: 'We kicked off and it was siling it down.' The appalling conditions have since been described in great detail. Tim Wilkinson and Ray Gent's *Rugby League In Its Own Words* concludes that the match should never have been played and hit the nail absolutely on the head. The players, they wrote, '…had to cope with a flooded Wembley surface that reduced scoring opportunities to a minimum as the ball either hydroplaned like a skimming stone or fell motionless like a grounded wrecking ball at the end of a shift.' Tony Hannan also summons up a fitting analogy, suggesting that, 'The saturated and slippery ball went to ground with frustrating regularity, where it stuck stubbornly to the sodden surface like a crouton on soup.'

The *Yorkshire Post*'s Alfred Drewry too raised serious questions about the players' safety in the terrible conditions in his report on the following Monday. 'Wembley was awash, so much so that one felt concerned whether the players' insurance against injury included the risk of death by drowning in the pools which covered the pitch.' Bev Risman had similar concerns. 'You only had to get involved in the first tackle to realise that there was something strange going on. In the first scrum, Tony Crosby's head went down and he was almost drowned in the front row.' The *Sunday Times* report the next day opened with making fun of what could have been a genuinely serious situation. 'Aye, son, thi Dad had a lovely death - he were drowned playing for Leeds in t'Cup final of 1968.'

Crosby confirms that drowning if a scrum collapsed was indeed a possibility and his main aim was to raise himself off the ground if he found himself pressed into the water. 'It was quite deep and when you went down, if you got your arm trapped you struggled to get up quick. It was difficult because it was scrum after scrum as the ball wasn't going in and it wasn't coming out.' Watching from the crowd, Crosby's wife, Kath, was unaware of the potentially serious implications of the conditions but remembers her impression of watching him. 'He just looked as though he was running from scrum to scrum. He'd get up from one and then there was another.' It is little surprise she gained that impression. There were a total of fifteen scrums in the first half alone which Crosby won by a margin of 11-4.

Trinity captain, Harold Poynton, was similarly perplexed by what was happening in front of him. 'I've never played in anything like it. I couldn't even stand up. Every time I got the ball I slipped, it was unreal.' And Poynton is in no doubt that the match should have been called off. 'I think it should have been, really, because it was that bad. It could have caused a lot of injuries. I mean, I got injured but I carried on. I went to tackle [Mick] Shoebottom and he slipped and hit me on the knee. It was quite bad for a minute or two and I carried it throughout the game.'

John Atkinson describes his experiences on the pitch that day as, 'like aquaplaning' and particularly remembers one incident involving Shoebottom. 'There's a picture somewhere of Mick. He went about twenty yards on his back with water going up at either side of him. I was looking round the crowd. I thought somebody might have 9.9 up!' David Jeanes also recalls the experience of continually going down onto the Wembley surface. 'Every time somebody tackled you, you went ten yards along the ground and finished up with a mouth full of all sorts of things.'

Barry Seabourne, as Leeds scrum-half, was at the heart of much of their play and had a key role as a tactical kicker but the conditions made his task almost impossible. 'In the first ten minutes or so we were under the posts in Wakefield's twenty-five and I went to have a drop at goal on the fourth [last] tackle. It didn't move so, of course, I couldn't kick the bloody thing. That would have been two points.'

Alfred Drewry's report offered a memorable description of his impressions of the match. 'The entertainment provided was a bizarre mixture of Laurel and Hardy slapstick and Wagnerian high drama [yes, thunder and lightning and all] although' he added, 'whether the principals appreciated the funny bits is doubtful.'

Ian Brooke describes the challenge of the playing surface that day. 'There were certain areas on the pitch that were absolutely perfect and other under, I would say, a good three or four inches of water. Sometimes the ball would just stop. Another would hit the puddle, aquaplane and just carry on, so you couldn't adjust yourself.'

'Both sides thought there's going to have to be a fair bit of kicking for territory,' recalls Bev Risman who was a master

Above: The referee's memorabilia donated to the Gillette Heritage Museum at the George Hotel, by controversial whistler John Hebblethwaite's family.
Below: Conditions more akin to front crawl than rugby league - John Atkinson, David Hawley, Barry Seabourne and referee Hebblethwaite look on.

Above: Wakefield's David Hawley and Ray Owen come to the assistance of Ken Batty as he is halted by Ray Batten and Bev Risman; Leeds' Barry Seabourne and Kenny Eyre in waiting.
Below: Harold Poynton, David Hawley and David Jeanes are photographed tackling a Leeds player amid the spray.

Above: (left to right) Ian Brooke, Pete Wilson, Mick Slater, Eddie Longley and Dave Cooper pictured in the Harewood Arms, Kirkgate, Wakefield, not long before we all boarded the midnight special to London

Left: The same gang, together with Roger Coupland and Ian Taylor, eat fish and chips at Westgate railway station. I'm in the middle raising the two-fingered salute

Above: Arriving at Tower Bridge early on the morning of the game, we have been joined by Ray Hensby and an unidentified fan we picked up on the way

Above: Albert Eyre, Ray Owen and Gary Cooper look on in disbelief as self-preservation in the tackle becomes the norm.

Below: A mess at the play the ball. John Atkinson marks Gary Cooper, as Bernard Watson scrambles past Matt McLeod to recover possession.

Above: Ray Batten and Tony Crosby (number 9) effect a tackle, while the fallen Alan Smith and George Shepherd watch intently.

Below: Ray Batten spins out a typical pass defying the conditions and cutting out Leeds halves Barry Seabourne and Mick Shoebottom, while David Jeanes tries to stop him and Don Fox looks worried.

Left and below: The respective post-match banquet menus; the winners felt deflated in unfamiliar surroundings while the losers partied the night away despite not winning the anticipated double.

Above: Leeds celebrate with pints in the dressing room - but not of beer, thanks to a sponsorship deal with the National Milk Council.

Right: Bev Risman takes the still dumbfounded Leeds players on the traditional lap of honour – by which time the rain had stopped.

Above: The return of the greats to the new Wembley in 2008. Neil Fox carries the Challenge Cup he missed out on in 1968, accompanied by Geoff Oakes - who was recovering from a broken leg that original day - and George Shepherd.

Above: Remembered on the big screen 40 years after his man of the match performance and tragic, last-gasp miss that settled the 'Watersplash' outcome.

of that art. 'Get them down on their own line and force them into making a mistake. In the first half it did start to dry out a little bit but every time, for example, Atki [John Atkinson] got the ball and went flying down the wing, when somebody tackled him, he skidded about twenty yards. And that was the same with me at full-back - you just had to do what you could.'

Sitting with the Trinity bench, Mick Morgan recalls that, after one particular scrum, the Wakefield hooker, George Shepherd was seen on the ground apparently searching in one of the many pools of water. 'Trailly said to Paddy [Armour, the Trinity physio] "Get on t'field. He's lost his contact lens." So Paddy ran on and all of a sudden George popped something in his mouth. He was looking for his chewing gum! Trailly said "Aren't we alright?" and turned the air even bluer.

The water wasn't just a problem for the players and match officials. Roger Ingham describes those facing the BBC's broadcasting crew. 'We were on the twenty-five at the end where the players came out. Only four rows from the front, we were getting a good view of all the happenings on the touchline. A cameraman came sprinting down the field when the play moved towards us, lost his legs and shot about forty yards down the touchline, like on a sledge. Then he had to go right back up the touchline to get his camera.' Ingham remembers another incident about five minutes later. 'Two cameramen finished up doing a Torvill and Dean. There was one on top of the other. It was hilarious.'

My own personal recollections of the eighty minutes are hazy and not just because of the lengthy passage of time since it took place. Among my gang it was the norm at that time to have a fair drop of beer before matches and the many hours we had been in London beforehand had given us ample opportunity to sink a good number of pints. George Denton, a Trinity fan at the match, reminded me that he and his pals, all of a similar age to myself, would frequently purchase Watney Party Sevens - large tins containing seven pints - and drink the entire contents, one each, before games. As a consequence, memories for a lot of us are limited because of the effects of alcohol, general tiredness from having been awake most of the previous night and the inevitable trips to the gents.

But there are a few points that remain with me. Predictably, apart from the unforgettable weather conditions, I have a clear recollection of the controversial refereeing decisions affecting my team, the two Wakefield tries and the incredible last seconds of the match. The early stages of the game indicated that goal kicks were likely to play a major role in determining the outcome. Bev Risman had put Leeds in front with a fine penalty within three minutes and shortly afterwards Don Fox equalised with a similarly excellent effort. The circumstances of that penalty constituted my first grievance with the referee. With Trinity playing towards the end I was at, Ken Hirst was dribbling the ball unopposed towards the Leeds line when, rather than allowing advantage, referee Hebblethwaite penalised the Loiners instead for obstruction. This decision in the first half, when Wakefield could well have scored, made it all the more difficult to accept his subsequent ruling in the second period to award a penalty try for a seemingly similar incident.

Risman put Leeds 4-2 ahead through a further penalty goal by the end of the first quarter. It was apparent by that point that if any tries were going to be scored, it was likely to be from loose balls being hacked on, as Ken Hirst had tried earlier, rather than from passing movements. It was one such which brought Hirst his first try after a slip by his opposing winger, John Atkinson. For Atkinson, the implications of the conditions that day were brought home when he attempted to prevent a long range Don Fox kick from crossing the touch-line as he defended the left wing in the Leeds half. 'In those days, you couldn't let a ball go into touch. I'm chasing it back thinking I can't afford to let it go because the forwards would give you a right rollocking. So I go to pick it up and the next thing I know I've kept the ball out of touch and I'm in the railings.'

Whereas the rules nowadays would give the defending side head and feed at the scrum if the ball went over the sideline in such circumstances, other than from a successful 40-20 kick, then the advantage would have gone to Trinity. 'I could just imagine what our pack would have been saying so I knew I had to get to that ball quickly and pick it up. Even if Kenny tackles me, we've got the ball. I couldn't do anything, I'd just no control. The next thing I know I'm in the dog track and looking at Kenny running away with the ball watching him score. There was nothing I could do about it. The minute I touched the ball, I just slid in the water.'

The *Rugby Leaguer*'s report of the incident the following week stressed that in more normal conditions Atkinson's efforts would have been commendable. 'He palmed the ball back infield as it was crossing the side-line, a feat that would have won praise on a dry ground for no other player was within 25 yards. Instead of making a quick recovery, the winger lost his footing and went down in a shower of spray.'

Atkinson's fellow winger, Alan Smith viewed the unfolding drama with horror on the opposite side. 'Kenny Hirst kicked it in a dead straight line and in those conditions the ball wouldn't bounce or deviate and he just dived on it. It's funny, because if something's going to happen like that, it'll be to John. But if he makes an error, then that's when he's at his most dangerous because he is just incensed then. He's possessed.' For Trinity fans that day, such a scenario came back to haunt them.

Don Fox had a difficult kick from a wide angle to convert the try but he succeeded, giving Wakefield a 7-4 lead. Conditions may have been bad at this point but they were to become much worse as the game moved towards half-time. With just over ten minutes left to play, clouds gathered overhead and the BBC recording shows a policeman at the side of the pitch putting on his overcoat as the heavens opened once again. As the half has just six minutes left to play, Eddie Waring in his commentary remarked that there was lightning as well and thunder can be heard. Just before the whistle went to end the opening forty minutes, he noted that hail was also coming down.

Chapter Eleven

Half-time

I have no idea how much I had to drink before the final but I do remember making a conscious decision to leave my place on the terrace and go to the toilet a short time before the inevitable half-time crush. It may have been my first visit to Wembley but I had heard stories of the mid point 'waterfalls' down the stadium steps and risked missing some of the on-field drama to avoid this particular spectacle. Although, with the weather conditions worsening, it was obvious that anything could happen in the second-half and the game could go either way, I felt with Trinity marginally in front, reasonably confident that we could go on to win. The Wakefield end was singing and in fairly good spirits at the interval.

It is noticeable, looking again at the television coverage, that as the half-time whistle is blown, the Wakefield players are first to return to the tunnel despite having defended the opposite end of the field in the first half. David Jeanes says as the weather appreciably worsened there was a thought that the game might not continue. 'All of us coming off as fast as we could was to get out of it and back into the warm, although wet, changing rooms, get a change of gear and sit down and talk about what we thought would go on.'

One press report notes referee Hebblethwaite stating that in places the water was nine inches deep and over his boot-tops. In an interview with Arthur Haddock of the *Yorkshire Evening Post* during the week following the match he indicated, however, that it had never entered into his reckoning to abandon the proceedings, saying, '…I could always see the lines.'

From my position high on the terraces at the tunnel end of the ground I distinctly recall that by half-time the area between the dead-ball line and the tunnel was almost entirely covered in standing water. One TV cameraman down below us was completely marooned and Barry Seabourne recalls ploughing through it. 'We almost had to swim back in. We were talking as we were going down the tunnel about what we could do to get in front. We discussed how Wakefield's try came about because Atki'd skidded.'

Atkinson himself describes the weather by now as being, 'completely out of control. I can remember Billy Ramsey saying, "I've never played in anything like this in all my life." The drama involving Atkinson when Hirst scored, was also referred to by coach Roy Francis as he warned the players about the conditions. Atkinson says he told his men to be thinking carefully about what they were doing. 'He said to us, "Don't be doing anything stupid that can put you under pressure. You've seen what's happened to Atki - how easily that can happen." He was telling us to play basic rugby.' That, though, was against his natural inclination.

Francis had had a discreet word with Atkinson about the incident leading to the try. 'Roy said to me, "Don't worry about that. You couldn't do anything about it. You did what you should have been doing." He reassured me not to be panicking about it.'

Syd Hynes took on board the half time message. 'The discussion was we're only one score behind. The game could go any way under the conditions. Just go out there and try the best you can because it was pointless saying do this or do that. And I suppose Wakefield got told the same.'

Most of Francis' motivational talks were pretty much the same concurs Alan Smith. 'He always inspired you with confidence and said, "The longer any game goes, the more you're going to win." He had a belief in the way we played and said, "Be patient, it'll come."'

Tony Crosby mentions that the Leeds squad changed their shorts for drier ones at half-time but remained in their same shirts as they only had one set of jerseys. He half expected to see Jack Myerscough in there. 'It wasn't unusual for the chairman to come into the dressing room at the half-way point and say, "We need the points boys; another ten quid."'

'It was just a matter of keep playing as you were,' was the message in the Trinity dressing room, according to Geoff Oakes. 'There was that much luck in it with the water that you couldn't make a plan. It just made it a bit of a farce in all fairness. You couldn't blame anybody or anything.'

Roger Ingham was also getting increasingly concerned about the monsoon. 'Just as they were going off at half-time, it come on like hell - hailstones, lightning, thunder, you name it. There was a lake by where the players got to the tunnel, where the dog track and the running track from the old Olympics was. It was an absolute lake. The band from the Guards were coming out in lashing rain and the leader marched straight through it, bold as brass. All the others followed and the crowd were jeering and cheering them, they were all over the place. You've never seen anything like it. And of course, there was that much rain coming down on top of their busbies, they couldn't see where they were going. I remember a guy near me saying, "It's better entertainment than t'match, this!" On leaving the field after their half-time renditions I could see David Jeanes begin to laugh as he came back out at a Guardsman who couldn't see where he was going and had walked into him.'

In his report of the match, Arthur Haddock remarked that 'In 30 Wembleys, it was the first time I'd seen the bandsmen surrounded by squads of workers.' The stadium groundsmen spent the half-time break forking the pitch to drain the water, as they had done before the match began. But they faced an absolutely impossible task and, as the second forty minutes was about to begin, the centre line gave the impression of a stream and there were huge puddles all over the field. On the terraces the consensus was that the pitch was unplayable but there was nobody among the group I was standing with who genuinely wanted the match abandoned. We were in front and pretty confident but none of us could have anticipated that we were about to witness events which would rank among the most dramatic and memorable in the history of sport.

Chapter Twelve

A controversial decision

Laws of the Game
Section 6, 3 (d)
Penalty try - the referee awards a penalty try which he may do if, in his opinion, a try would have been scored but for the unfair play of the defending team. A penalty try is awarded between the goalposts irrespective of where the offence occurred.

It probably didn't strike anybody at the time but it was the 68th minute of the 68th final in'68. The superstitious would say something probably had to happen and it certainly did. It was an incident that divided opinion on the day and has done so ever since. There was little to remark upon during the early stages of the second half but, with the weather conditions even worse following the half-time downpour, two sides still committed to throwing the ball around were inevitably making numerous errors.

The build-up to the controversy is fairly straightforward,

starting with a Barry Seabourne punt towards Trinity's right wing in the Wakefield half. Winger Ken Hirst appears to have the kick covered, running back to where he anticipates the ball will bounce. But it lands in a puddle and holds up. He tries to stop near to where the ball has sopped but slips to the ground. His opposing winger John Atkinson hoofs the ball forward towards the Wakefield posts. Ken Batty, Trinity's left winger, sprints cross field but, as he attempts to cover the ball, Atkinson hacks on again and is seen to come in contact with Trinity centre Gert Coetzer, as he veers it to the right of the posts. Referee Hebblethwaite is seen pointing to between the posts and signalling that Wakefield had offended by pushing the Leeds player.

Atkinson is clear what happened. 'I kicked and I'm chasing it. The surprising thing was that the ball hit the pitch and it stopped. It didn't bounce either way. I thought, 'this is great'. I could see Kenny [Batty] coming across so I kicked it again and it goes to the line. I knew I was quicker than them to get there. Next thing I know, somebody's got hold of me, pulling me. I think I slipped as a result of it. I remember thinking it was a waste.'

But the incident was by no means over as Atkinson continues. 'Next thing, the referee's penalising and Bev says, "He's given us a try!" I didn't even know, I'd never been awarded an obstruction try before in my life. You didn't see that many. They were coming at different angles and Coetzer was behind me.' Interestingly, Atkinson had been under the impression for many years that it was Batty, and not the chasing Coetzer, who was directly involved in the incident but it was the South African who can be clearly seen in the television footage tangling with him. Coetzer was quoted in Eddie Waring's *Sunday Mirror* report as strongly denying any obstruction. 'I was staggered when I heard the ref was awarding the try against me. I never touched him.' In the *Sunday People* he added, 'I got to the ball first and Atkinson bumped off me. The ball broke loose and Ian Brooke picked it up. I couldn't believe it when the referee gave a try because Brooke would have beaten Atkinson to the ball anyway.'

Barry Seabourne was near to the action and is clearly of the opinion Atkinson would have scored had he not been impeded. 'I kicked the ball deep into the twenty-five and it stuck in the water. John hacked it on then, right across the field. He saw the cover coming across and kicked the other way from where the Wakefield players were coming. It went over the try line and he was there, and I don't know who it was who pushed him and he went flying. From where I was, the next one following up, I clearly saw him being pushed. Basically, John was first there.'

Ken Eyre was also in a good position to see what happened. 'It unfurled in front of me, we kicked the ball and John hared after it. He was one of the paciest wingers, not just in British rugby, in the world. There weren't many Australians could outrun Atki with his pace and Coetzer got in his way.' Ken's brother Albert, also in the vicinity, agrees. 'It was a try. When I've watched it back I've always thought it was the right decision.' Syd Hynes' view is that, 'It was a good decision under the conditions. He got chopped off, did Atki, and the referee didn't hesitate. He went straight between the sticks and gave an obstruction try.'

Tony Crosby regards the award as a courageous decision. 'I wouldn't like to have been in his shoes refereeing that match and to give that. It was anybody's ball. I think we got away there a little bit in all honesty. We were very grateful. It was a fifty-fifty call. Anyway, we got it and that's what matters!'

Atkinson's grim resolve in pursuit of Seabourne's kick

came as no surprise to Alan Smith, especially as it made up for his disappointment in the Hirst try. 'That was the determination of Atkinson, the pace and his view that he was going to get a decision. He'd score tries when we needed them. He forced the issue. He made the play. He made everybody sit up. He was that determined and he obviously convinced Mr Hebblethwaite that he was going to get there. In those ten years he was the best winger in our game.

'But it was under dubious circumstances. The decision went for us. Any sportsman will tell you that if you are on the field and you get the decision, great. And if you don't get it, you can't do anything about it. Nobody could say it was the right one. Under those conditions, there's so many variations, today, with the screen, it would have been 'no try' wouldn't it?'

The media's view reflected heated debate and differing perspectives. Eddie Waring's reaction during his commentary was, 'Well, that was the most sensational happening in a Cup final for a long, long while, whatever the conditions.' In his *Yorkshire Evening Post Sport's Echo* report on the evening of the match, Arthur Haddock noted that Leeds had gone ahead, '…with what will go down as one of the most controversial tries in Wembley history.' Waring subsequently wrote that, 'As he [Atkinson] chased after the ball towards the line, four Wakefield players combined to stop him touching down.' The *Daily Mail*'s Brian Batty suggested, 'Television recordings clearly show that winger Atkinson was obstructed but leave grave doubts whether he could have beaten opposing centres Coetzer and Brooke to touch down.' Noting that referee Hebblethwaite had been in no doubt Atkinson would have scored, Alan Smith in the *Daily Sketch* added, 'I think a dozen other referees could easily have been divided in their support for and against him.'

The award of an obstruction try went surprisingly unremarked in John Huxley's detailed history of the Challenge Cup, but others recalling Mr Hebblethwaite's decision were a good deal less non-committal. Trinity's Chairman, John Ridge, was livid over the ruling. 'How could anyone award an obstruction try in conditions like that when players were slipping and sliding? It was disgraceful,' he argued in the *Wakefield Express*.

Their correspondent John Allen wrote, 'The contentious point arose over whether referee John Hebblethwaite....was not overgenerous in awarding a try? The Leeds winger had still a fair distance to travel on turf so treacherous that it had toppled many players when moving at little above walking pace.' Allen pointed out the inconsistency between the award of the obstruction try to Atkinson and the earlier one on Ken Hirst which led to a penalty goal. 'Has it been so easily overlooked by so many that as early as the fifth minute, Hirst was obstructed as he chased a loose ball with what appeared to be about an equal chance of scoring as Leeds winger Atkinson had later on?...If the referee had delayed his stop signal to allow Hirst to take an advantage, he might easily have gone on to score' he continued.

This same point was made the following week in a strongly worded protest about the refereeing of the match published in the *Rugby Leaguer*. A P. Norris of Ossett wrote that, 'The incident where Wakefield had possession after a foul by Leeds, and had a completely open run to score under the posts was the turning point. Referee Hebblethwaite did not apply the advantage rule, blew for the foul and gave Wakefield a penalty kick.'

Surprisingly, perhaps, one of the Wakefield players supports the referee's interpretation of events in the initial incident. Ian Brooke, as Hirst's centre partner, was close to the action.'Kenny kicked it and got obstructed by Atkinson. From my point of view, the ball went just like a rocket, hit some water and just aquaplaned and went dead. It didn't stop in the in-goal area so, to give Mr. Hebblethwaite his due, and under those circumstances, I've no grievance at all about that. As far as I was concerned it was a fair decision.'

The Wakefield players were no so forgiving about the later - and I would say, defining - incident. John Lindley's historical account of Trinity from the club's formation up to 1973 contained a detailed description of what went through the minds of the Trinity faithful at the time of the fateful 68th minute incident. He wrote that, '… they were thinking of Hirst's unfortunate slipped foothold, of Batty's failure to 'kill' the ball, and they were thinking too of how a decision which hinges on some 'certainty of scoring' could be made under the prevailing conditions which made everything, except falling and losing possession, extremely doubtful let alone 'certain'.'

In his description of the 1968 final in Harold Poynton's benefit brochure, Lindley had argued that what he termed, 'the real point of destiny' came not in the last seconds but, '… in the 68th minute when Leeds were awarded the try they had found impossible to score through their own ability against this Trinity defence.' He rationalised the situation in a way so many others had done subsequent to the match. 'If that try, and the resultant conversion, had levelled the scores [instead of altering the lead] few would have quibbled with a drawn outcome however hard they found it to agree with the actual award.'

While Ian Brooke clearly sided with John Hebblethwaite's fifth minute decision to award Wakefield a penalty for the obstruction by Atkinson, rather than a penalty try, to this day he fiercely contests the award of the obstruction try to Atkinson during the second half. His is a detailed recollection of the incident from his ideal vantage point. 'Coetzer and Atkinson were running side-by-side. I was at an angle, coming in from the left hand side and I saw them both together and neither pushed the other.'

Referee Hebblethwaite's perception of the incident, later reported in the *Sunday Express*, was somewhat different. 'I never had any doubts that he was obstructed. I'm not bothered with names, there were just Wakefield jerseys and a Leeds jersey and the Leeds player was both pushed and then his jersey was grabbed. I only go by the colour of a team's jersey, not by names. I know a Leeds player was pushed and then his jersey grabbed from behind. I have seen the incident re-run twice on TV and it confirms my decision.'

As the subsequent decision to award an obstruction try to Leeds was based on the referee's view that Coetzer had impeded Atkinson, Brooke's impression that neither had pushed one another is interesting. He describes what he believed happened as, 'an accidental coming together' and expands on the point. 'They were that close to one another that, as they were running - and they were both pumping with their arms - their arms interlocked. They both just parted slightly.' Harold Poynton recalls, 'The ball was all over the place - slipping and sliding - then they just came together. That was my opinion, I thought he's blown for a knock-on or something.'

The referee determined that, had Coetzer not, in his view, obstructed Atkinson, the Leeds player was likely to have touched the ball down over the line. Brooke points out that, because of his position at that point, that would not have happened. 'The ball, under the conditions, instead of going flying into dead stopped on the try line and I was first to the ball. The angle I was running at was from, I'd come across from behind the posts, as they were running towards them, was from the right centre position and as I picked the ball up they were both about a yard off. They were on the try line itself. The ball was in the middle of the in-goal area. I came and picked the ball up. As I picked it up, I came out in-between both posts and I got to about ten yards and the whistle had gone.'

Brooke was mystified by the referee whistling at that point. 'I couldn't understand what the whistle had gone for. When I looked round and realised Mr. Hebblethwaite was pointing to the try line, I couldn't believe it because I thought he'd made a bad decision. To me, I knew I was going to be first to the ball. To me, he'd given a try because he thought Atkinson was going to score, or get there before Coetzer. He probably would have done but I'd have beaten Atkinson to the ball. To me that was the sole thing. I was going to be first to the ball and it was a wrong decision.'

David Jeanes is even more vehement. 'I couldn't possibly see how he could give a try because, in any circumstances it would be contentious, in those it was unbelievable. As rugby league players you accept what's gone on. Afterwards, you might feel bitter about it and I think a lot of people actually did. It was ridiculous, absolutely ridiculous.'

On the sidelines, there was an understandable reaction from the Trinity bench. 'We all went mad,' says Geoff Oakes. 'It was a bad decision. Had they had television replays like they do now, the referee would have been castigated. It wasn't an obstruction try.' He recalls coach Ken Traill's reaction. 'He did have a few words to say! He was quite good at getting excited.' Mick Morgan, alongside Oakes on the Wakefield bench, regards the awarding of the try as, 'the worst decision ever in rugby league.' He says, 'If you look at the laws of the game, it says you've got to be one hundred per cent sure a try's going to be scored. Now, on that day, you couldn't be one hundred per cent sure you'd got your own boots on, never mind a try's going to be scored. That was absolutely bonkers. And Leeds couldn't believe it. Nobody could believe it. Nobody knew what the decision was, even the Leeds players.'

Peter Fox, watching on in alarm, qualifies his comments on the referee's decision by also making the not unreasonable point that John Hebblethwaite lacked the technology available to today's officials who can refer an incident for an independent look at the video evidence. But, nevertheless, he is strongly critical of the award. 'The thing was, he gave the try against the laws of the game. He'd got to be certain the try would have been scored before he could allow it as an obstruction try and he didn't do that, clearly. He made a mistake there. Why, I don't know, but he made a mistake. Brookey had got to the ball before either Atki or Coetzer so I don't know how the referee could come to his decision. His refereeing in the match - I'd no qualms about it - until that obstruction try.'

Fox's brother, Neil, also focuses on the question of certainty of scoring. 'The referee can't give an obstruction try unless he is definitely sure that the player would have scored, and there was no way Atkinson was going to score. You couldn't guarantee him to score. I know Coetzer and him were pulling each and bumping each other on the way to the ball but on the last kick ahead the man who came away with it on the try-line was Ian Brooke. Ian would have beaten either of them to the ball anyway. As he came away, we couldn't believe that the referee had pulled him up and given an obstruction try.'

From his position high in the stand helping with the

television commentary, Ken Rollin was much further from the incident than those on the field but, despite being at that stage very firmly in the Leeds camp has a clear opinion about the incident. 'My first reaction was it's no try, but it could be a penalty. When the referee indicated a try I was absolutely amazed. Again, of course, when you see it three or four times it looks totally different but I still say it wasn't a try, after all this time.'

The referee's decision was, not surprisingly, challenged at the time by Trinity. Brooke states, 'We just told him in no uncertain terms that we didn't think it was a try. We thought he'd got the decision wrong and we couldn't understand how he'd come to it and wanted an explanation. But he just wouldn't talk to us. But having experienced Mr. Hebblethwaite over the season, he was one of those guys who never talked to you anyway. You could have a chat with Thomas, D.T.H. Davies. All the other refs you used to get on with great and you talked to them, called them 'Sir'. Everybody makes mistakes but never, with Mr. Hebblethwaite, did you get any banter at all.'

Writing in the *Rugby Leaguer* a week after the final, 'Left Footer' the paper's Trinity correspondent, who many years later I discovered had been local Catholic Priest Father Cornelius Finn, suggested that when men gathered years ahead they would still dispute the penalty try. 'Everyone I spoke to at Wembley could not understand why the referee gave such a decision. True, some said: 'Maybe a penalty goal, but certainly not a penalty try.' It is no secret to say that the players on both sides were equally surprised by the referee's decision.'

While it was hardly surprising that the local Wakefield newspaper, Lindley, Trinity's historian, and 'Left Footer' should draw attention to such inconsistencies, it is worthy of note that the Leeds-based *Yorkshire Post* also raised considerable doubts about the obstruction try decision. Its correspondent, Alfred Drewry, reported that, 'The justice of Mr. J. P. Hebblethwaite's award of a try to Atkinson was bitterly contested. The referee [and Atkinson naturally] were both convinced that Atkinson would have reached the ball first had not Coetzer impeded him. Brooke maintained stoutly that he had his hand on the ball at the time, so as far as the award of a try was concerned whatever happened between the other two players was irrelevant. Penalty perhaps; try definitely not. Mr. Hebblethwaite's decision surprised me, but he was a lot better placed to see what happened than I was.'

Drewry's colleague at the *Yorkshire Evening Post*, Arthur Haddock, took a similar view. 'It has', he suggests, 'been established that the winger [Atkinson] was impeded near the posts, but it remains a matter of opinion whether he would have been able to reach the ball over the line. I though a penalty kick, worth two points, would have met the offence in such conditions.' The *Huddersfield Daily Examiner*'s report of the match proffered, '...Wakefield might with some justification have felt that at one point they were being robbed of the RL Challenge Cup...' Their correspondent, The Scout, added, '...I must admit that this seemed to me a harsh decision as it did not appear that Atkinson had any real chance of scoring.'

The writer Geoffrey Moorhouse deemed the incident so significant he singled it out for reference in his official centenary history of rugby league. 'The obstruction leading to the try...had almost certainly been unintentional, because by then it was virtually impossible for anyone to keep his feet in what would be remembered as the Watersplash final.' Tony Hannan described the award of a try as, 'one of the most controversial refereeing decisions that Wembley has ever seen…,' suggesting that 'To widespread bewilderment, York referee J Hebblethwaite decreed that Atkinson had been deliberately pushed off the ball…'

In his biography of Don Fox, Ron Bailey, a life-long Featherstone Rovers supporter, claimed, 'From the evidence, both Coetzer and Atkinson were guilty of obstructing each other, but neither could have reached the ball over the line. It was a hugely contentious decision, but the referee did not have the benefit of a 'video referee' in those days, and could only make the decision on his interpretation.'

Interestingly, even some of the Leeds players were somewhat taken aback by the awarding of an obstruction try. Bev Risman recalls, 'I was surprised by the decision. I could see that something had gone on and Atki, in a way, had been impeded but my immediate impression was shock when he actually gave the penalty try. I had assumed that I would be kicking a penalty from in front of the posts. I saw the incident, it looked innocuous. It was an obstruction in some small way and, therefore, something had to be given. But when he gave the penalty try, I was thrilled to bits.'

Attempting a balanced perspective was the *Sunday Express*'s Jack Bentley. He wrote, 'It is ridiculous to say, as some people did, that Wakefield were robbed because Leeds winger John Atkinson was awarded an obstruction try… Many rugby-wise folk who watched the game on television have told me they agreed with John Hebblethwaite's decision.' Alan Thomas of the *Daily Express* was of the same view. He concluded, 'York referee John Hebblethwaite, central figure in the most controversial incident I have ever seen at Wembley, was right,' noting that the decision had led Leeds coach Roy Francis to label him, 'the bravest man at Wembley.' Thomas continued, 'Even with a magnificent view from the Press Box I would not have been prepared to say on Saturday that Atkinson was obstructed. But the on-the-spot referee, who had a five-star match in the difficult conditions, had no hesitation in giving the try.'

Francis did indeed praise Hebblethwaite's courage for taking the decision against a background of tremendous pressure in such a final. He told the *Daily Sketch*, 'Today we have seen Hebblethwaite move into the giant class as a referee. It took a big, big man to make that decision in a Wembley Cup final.' Perhaps unsurprisingly, Francis's opposite number, Ken Traill, had a different view of the incident, telling them 'I cannot understand how it was an obstruction try. As far as I could see the ball was not even over the line.' He told the *Daily Mail* he had support of his view from Leeds official [and former player] Arthur Clues who, he claimed, said, 'I did not think it was a try. But it was one of those decisions that if it had been for you then you would take it. As it was, we got it.'

Hebblethwaite's son David says that, despite all the controversy around the decision, for his father, 'It was as clear as a bell. It was definitely an obstruction in his mind. He didn't even think of the conditions. Coetzer pushed Atkinson and that was it.' The *Rugby Leaguer*'s 'Lancastrian' came to a similar conclusion arising from the TV replay. 'As three or more players all moving helter-skelter were involved in the Atkinson obstruction try, it was difficult to reach a quick decision from the lofty press box. A study of the BBC film, however, clearly vindicates Referee Hebblethwaite. Atkinson was first pushed yards short of the line and grabbed by the arm when each player was going for the touch down.' 'Lancastrian' referred to Wakefield's anger over this decision, cautioning the club on their response: 'Wakefield's threat to protest against the decision is misplaced. In recent seasons they have had the benefit of decisions of this nature. Against St. Helens, in last season's Championship final at Headingley, Ginger Owen was awarded an obstruction try that was hotly disputed.'

A letter in the same edition of the newspaper from a T. J. Aked in Whitby made a similar point. In attacking Trinity Chairman, John Ridge's, criticism of the obstruction try he wrote, 'I must remind Mr. Ridge that he was perfectly willing to accept a similar controversial try awarded to Wakefield in last season's Championship final, which was played in equally bad conditions.'

Also writing in the edition, correspondent 'Left Footer' appeared to foresee the eventual use of television video recordings to accurately determine on-field rulings. He wrote, '…with the advent of TV video tape and a re-run of the incident , the position can be definitely decided…' If one was to fast-forward this incident to a contemporary live TV broadcast of a game there is little doubt that a video referee would note some pushing and pulling between Atkinson and Coetzer. But the key issue in any replay would surely be the point raised by the *Yorkshire Post*'s Alfred Drewry. Although Wakefield's Ian Brooke gathered the ball from behind the line and ran it out of defence did he have it covered and would he have got to it at the time Atkinson and Coetzer were entangled?

Drewry, interestingly, in the editorial, noting the extensive debate over what television news features of the match had shown of the incident, called for the game to be shown again. 'Most followers who have seen the BBC re-runs of the Atkinson obstruction try have been able to draw their own conclusions. Many staying in London for the weekend or travelling North did not see the programme. Perhaps the BBC could help to settle a thousand arguments by another showing.'

When the award of an obstruction try registered with Wakefield supporters, the bulk of whom were at the end of the ground where it happened, a wave of booing greeted the decision. My initial thoughts, from the terracing at the tunnel end, was that Ian Brooke had been deemed to touch the ball down. It took some time for the referee's pointing to between the posts in front of us to be fully understood and, at first, it seemed consistent with him indicating a Wakefield drop-out. I had watched and played rugby league for the best part of a decade at this point and could only recall seeing obstruction tries being awarded on a couple of occasions. Inevitably too, Wembley finals attract those who are not regular attenders at ordinary matches and they must have been completely baffled by what was unfolding.

Harry Jepson's view of the incident is that it was absolutely par for the course that day. 'The situation which led up to it, with so many unforgettable things happening, I think the referee had a desire to keep the game moving. I was disappointed when the try was given but I didn't criticise the referee, it was one of dozens of other things which could have been equally significant in deciding the result. It was a try which was in accord with the curious things that happened throughout the 80 minutes. It really was because there was nothing clear about anything.'

The contentious 68th minute alone could have provided the main talking point of the final for time immemorialbut the remaining twelve were to throw up even more dramatic twists and turns.

Chapter Thirteen

The last seconds that live forever

As the game neared full-time, with Leeds in front by two points, Trinity were penalised. Barry Seabourne takes up the events. 'I got the ball and was coming away from acting half-back ready to put Albert Eyre through, and I got stiff-armed. I think it was Matt McLeod who did it.' The DVD of the BBC broadcast indicates that McLeod was indeed involved in the tackle but so was Trinity captain, Harold Poynton, and it was he who was deemed to have committed the foul.

Seabourne continues, 'The referee gave us a penalty and so Bev says to Clarkie, "I'll kick the goal." I thought that if I'd been captain I wouldn't have done it because the referee had said it was more or less time.' Seabourne's view is that Leeds should at that point have kicked for touch. 'There was no way Wakefield were going to come the length of the field. Bev was a left-footed kicker, kicking to the right hand side, and he would have found touch in their twenty-five, so we would have been stationed there for three tackles and I'd have put the ball out. That's where the ball should have gone.'

Risman thought that, with conditions so difficult underfoot, if he missed it from that distance - as seemed likely - at least he would put the ball dead and Leeds would get it back. Somewhat unbelievably, he hit it sweetly and it sailed over to make it 11-7.

After Risman's goal, Trinity scrum-half Ray Owen placed the ball on the centre-spot for the re-start as both sets of forwards lined up on his left. Unbeknown to the Leeds defence, Don Fox had had a quite word with winger Ken Hirst. Hirst, many years later, told Norman Hazell, 'Don said, 'Get ready. When I kick off, start running.'

Fox told *Daily Express* reporter Jack Bentley at the time what his thinking had been in those last few seconds. 'I knew it was no good kicking to the Leeds forwards with so little time to go.' Some observers - including contemporary editions of the *Huddersfield Daily Examiner* have suggested that the try Hirst scored from the kick off was also somewhat disputed but Risman, close to what happened, had no such doubts. 'I've got no grumbles about the touchdown. It was about us not stopping it. I was totally devastated.'

He said that the Leeds players had expected the final whistle straight after his successful penalty. 'Mr. Hebblethwaite - God bless his soul - had basically said it was full-time. When I kicked the penalty I thought it's all over, he'll blow for full-time. Then, to my surprise, he didn't. When we got the penalty we specifically asked him, 'Is it full-time?' and he'd said, 'It's just about full-time.' To me that implied once I'd taken the kick that would be it. That's why we opted to go for goal, to kill the game. We didn't anticipate a situation where they came all the way back up to the halfway line and got a final shot, which made all the difference really.'

Ian Brooke says the Trinity players had heard the dialogue between one of their opponents and the referee and understood that there was about a minute to go as Ray Owen restarted the game. 'So Ray Owen comes and is putting the ball down, Harold is at the side of him, and I'm stood with them because I was going to run upfield, straight up the centre line. Kenny was really wide out on the touchline. Unbeknown to me, Don had said to Kenny, behind the posts, "Stay wide out - I'm going to kick it to your side this time." We didn't know till afterwards.' Poynton confirms that he, even as the Trinity captain, knew nothing of Fox's intentions.

Even Owen, who was about to take the kick-off was unaware of Fox's intentions. Brooke remembers, 'I'm stood at the side of Ray and he's putting the ball down and going to kick it to the left-hand side where all the Leeds players were. Then Don says, "I'm kicking it this side." Ray replied, "You what?" and Don repeats, "I'm gonna kick it to this side" and, as soon as Ray's put the ball down, Don did.'

In his commentary position, Ken Rollin had concluded by then that Leeds, had almost certainly won the Cup. 'The only danger now is that Trinity get the ball. The odds are ninety per cent that Leeds will get the ball back and it's finished at that stage. Then, typical Don; great brain, brilliant footballer. They were coming to the half-way line and suddenly I watched him coming in and I'm thinking, my goodness, he's going to kick it the other side. One of the Leeds players put their foot down and the ball went straight underneath it. At that stage, when I saw that, the commentator said to me, "What now?"'

Rollin speaks of having a conversation with Fox and Ray Owen about this re-start at a dinner at Painthorpe Country Club in Wakefield, many years later. Fox recalled that Owen actually wouldn't take the kick-off. 'Because they said it was time, Ray wouldn't kick-off so Don did it. Don said to him something like, "You wouldn't bloody kick-off anyway." And then he thought it's better to kick to the other side, which he did.'

Brooke describes what happened as, 'a miraculous try scored under miraculous conditions.' Hirst had chased Fox's fooling re-start, kicked the ball forward himself and dived on it to score a remarkable try to reduce the margin to 11-10 and Brooke reckons that if Hirst had had twenty more goes he wouldn't be able to repeat his amazing feat that day. 'It was different from being a dry day. A rugby ball's awkward as it is, with it rolling, but under those conditions, there were about two or three puddles down the right hand side. And there was one about ten to fifteen yards from the try-line which was massive. I think Atki slipped in that one.'

Atkinson vividly remembers his feelings over those last seconds as cup final victory appeared to have suddenly turned to heartbreaking defeat. 'The ball's coming towards Bernard Watson and I, and I'm watching it, and thinking we're alright. Again, I could see Kenny is chasing the ball, it hits the floor and Bernard puts his foot down to trap the ball. It went straight under his foot and, next thing we know, "oh Christ," they've scored.

'I was not in a position to get anywhere near the ball. Kenny's past us and, I thought, of all places to score, they're right under the posts. All I could think was, "that's it. We've lost it. We've lost the final."' Albert Eyre was in the same frame of mind, 'We thought we were obviously on our way until the Kenny Hirst try. What I remember about it is everything seemed to be in slow motion, there was no speed about it.'

His brother Ken had lined up with his fellow forwards on the opposite side of the field to Atkinson to defend Ray Owen's anticipated kick-off and could do nothing. 'Don just cleverly switched the kick and then it was like a comedy of errors to be quite honest. We're on the right hand side of the field and all this is happening on the left. You start trotting across because you think the play's going to start from over there, but it didn't because of Kenny Hirst. All I saw was him fly-hacking the ball, it stopping dead, Bernard Watson falling on it and missing it and somebody else missing it. I think Shoey [Mick Shoebottom] got across there and it evaded him. It stopped in front of Bev and Ken kicked it again so Bev then had to turn round, it was just unbelievable.'

Barry Seabourne's instinct about kicking to touch, rather than going for goal, appeared to have been right as he watched what then happened. 'We were just getting back into position and Bernard Watson went onto the ten yard line. We used to split the field up. I used to drop back sometimes to catch the ball to feed the forwards. Wakefield kicked off - took a short one. He went down to get it did Watty and missed it. They hacked it on. Bev came across to take it and missed it. They hacked it on over the line and scored. That was the finish. Wakefield had won as far as I was concerned. We couldn't believe it. There was the goal to be kicked but, really, Don couldn't miss it.'

Alan Smith pinpoints Fox's brilliance in setting up that final try. 'Don Fox - clever footballer. The lad's still thinking. The game was full of them then. All the time probing, looking left, looking right, keeping his eyes open. The ball just skimmed under Watson's boot and stopped. It was same again as the first try: Hirst kicked it, a perfect kick - he ought to have been a soccer player - and it went dead straight. I started to run across and you could see others braking and sliding. They were all missing trying to get to that ball. Down they went and Ken kicked it again and it went straight again and it stopped right behind the sticks. It was like slow motion. And the referee's straight up - a try!' Smith had no doubt at that point that the Challenge Cup was going to

Wakefield. 'I thought, that's it. Game over. After Bev's goal we thought we had won it. And I couldn't believe it, another twist. That's it. It's over.'

Albert Eyre recalls his feelings as the Leeds players lined up on the try line behind the posts for Fox's kick. 'I thought we'd had it. Stood under the sticks with Kenny I was just exhausted. The position where it was, it was all over and done with because Don never missed many goal kicks. I just thought we'd had it. I'm on my knees. Kenny was stood one side, Billy Ramsey was at the other. I was just exhausted. My whole body was saying, "Well, that's it" basically.'

Tony Crosby was similarly resigned to defeat at that point. 'Foxy didn't miss goals, not in front of the posts. If you look back, I was kneeling down and I think I was praying at the time, never expecting him to miss. I just could not see him missing that.' Mind you, even at such a dramatic moment, Crosby's was a typical Yorkshireman's prayer. 'I'd dressed my wife up and it had been an expensive week. I needed the winning money.'

Many of those who played in this match have relived those final moments through the television footage since. John Atkinson says, 'Well, if you see the picture, I'm on my wing and I'm on my hands and knees facing away from everything. I could hear Bernard swearing because he thought he'd made a mistake.'

On the other side, David Jeanes recalls how his own emotions suddenly changed in a matter of seconds. 'It was knowing there was about a minute to go and we'd basically lost the game, come what may. We didn't know - or I didn't know - what Don was going to do. You watch the video. You'll see some big, silly lad come bounding in, jumping up and down after the try and that's me. All I could think was, "fantastic, how on earth have we done that?"'

Two words summed up Ken Eyre's simultaneous feelings at that point. 'Just sick, the previous eighty minutes flashed my mind wondering, "What the hell have we done. Why did we do this?" You're looking at each other but nobody can speak.' But, according to Eyre, somebody eventually did as Fox prepared to convert Hirst's try. 'I stood at the side of the posts and can vividly remember Mick Clark shouting to him "Miss it!" Definitely. Mick Clarke shouted "Miss it!" Mick, as captain, was going up for the Cup. He was entitled to shout.'

What was going through Fox's mind as he stepped forward to take that kick can now only be imagined. It is clear, however, that he had spoken earlier of his hope that he would not be faced with such a scenario. Fox's son, Greg, is aware of a television interview done by his father some years after the match in which he recalled his dad saying to his wife, Mary, before the final that he hoped he wouldn't have to decide the result. In the event, that was precisely how it turned out.

Conversations around the ground during the incredible drama of these last seconds are recalled by many who were there that day. According to the *Daily Sketch*, in the Royal Box the Leeds Chairman Jack Myerscough was seated alongside the Prime Minister and he related that Harold Wilson had congratulated him on victory just before the last few moments of the game. After the Wakefield try under the posts Myerscough said to Wilson, 'That's shattered it.' Wilson replied 'Keep calm. I have seen kicks like that missed in both union and rugby league.' Seated on the Wakefield bench, Mick Morgan says, 'The most famous line ever was when everybody jumped up when Hirsty scored the try, Trailly says, "Sit down. He hasn't kicked the effin' goal yet." Everybody had just jumped up because it was time and we'd won the Cup. When Don missed it, well, you couldn't talk. We were just numb.'

Longstanding Wakefield fan Roy Thackrah, who has been the club's timekeeper for a number of years, remembers a story told by John Fawcett, his old boss at Wakefield engineering firm British Jeffrey Diamond, of what happened where he was in the crowd after Hirst scored that final try. 'There had been banter with a nearby Leeds fan throughout the match. As the try was scored, and Trinity looked to have won the match, he ruffled this chap's hair and his wig fell off into a puddle! He picked it up and tried to put it back onto his head with water running down his face. He was so embarrassed he never spoke to the surrounding fans again, even when his team finally took the Cup.'

Seated behind the Wakefield bench, Neil Fox remembers how he felt at the crucial moment. 'I couldn't believe that we could score a minute before the finish of the game. And then everyone jumped up. The crowd was excited, thinking we'd won. I thought we'd won because I thought Don would have kicked the goal. But when it all calmed down a bit, I'm sat there thinking this is a kick that I wouldn't have liked to take. It is one of the most pressurised kicks ever - the last kick of the match to win a Cup final. I just leant back in my chair and thought I wish it was me who was taking this, not for the glamour, but because I was thinking that, if anything goes wrong, Don is a bit of a worrier. The people around me were saying "We've won! We've won!" And I'm thinking, "not yet." I was desperate for him to kick it, but I didn't know, because I wouldn't have liked to kick goals in those conditions.'

Other brother Peter, seated with Norman Hazell and their party, remembers that, as Hirst scored, 'everybody - Norman and all the lads with me - were up in the air. I'm thinking the game's not over yet because the goal's got to be kicked. The thing that disappointed me most was that all the Wakefield players and the reserves on the bench were up - like all the spectators - thinking the game's over. The Leeds players had their hands on their heads assuming the game's over the other way, that they'd lost it. And I'm thinking - I must have been the only rational person in the stadium - it's not over because the goal's got to be kicked.'

Hazell reflects, 'I thought we've won the Cup, although actually we were losing 11-10. Peter Fox reached up and put his hand on my shoulder - he was sitting beside me. "Sit down Norman," he said. "He hasn't kicked it yet." I said, "Oh, but come on Peter." Peter says, "Wait Norman, wait. He hasn't kicked it yet."' Hazell wasn't alone in believing it was all over and Wakefield had won. Down on the field, Ian Brooke as he walked back to the halfway line was sure he was on the winning team and Poynton recalls being convinced, 'He'll kick it - and we'll win.'

For David Atkinson, like Hazell another former Wakefield Mayor, those final moments are etched forever in his memory. 'We were in a large group of Wakefield supporters and were naturally elated that Trinity seemed to have snatched the win after all that had happened and when Don was preparing to kick the goal everyone was jumping up and down assuming victory. I foolishly thought I ought to point out that he hadn't kicked it yet. Minutes later I watched in disbelief as he missed the goal from in front of the posts and a tearful lady turned to me and stated very loudly that it was my fault.'

Brian Robinson, a teacher at Rothwell Secondary School at the time and Trinity supporter, had brought a coach load of pupils down. 'Our final try was wonderful. I jumped high in the air in celebration and said something and one of the schoolboys commented, "Did you hear what Robbo said?" Perhaps in my excitement I had uttered a comment which was totally unprofessional for a teacher to say in front of his kids, but fortunately I never did discover which word had slipped out.'

Robinson also remembers having a premonition of what was to follow after the try. 'For a brief moment time seemed to stand still and, when I was up in the air, a terrible thought crossed my mind. I was sure we would miss the kick at goal. I then did something I have never done before or since. I have often refused to take the game too seriously as there are more important things in life but, on this occasion, I turned my back on the pitch. I just couldn't watch the kick at goal. The crowd told me what I had already expected, the whistle went and it was all over.'

Robert Smith, in his early teens and supporting the Loiners, has a clear recollection of the feelings of his group of Leeds fans as it appeared that Hirst's second try had prised the Challenge Cup from their grasp. 'We were all devastated as it seemed the Cup was not going to be ours after all, with Don Fox set to kick the easiest conversion you can imagine. We were directly behind the posts. My friends couldn't look but I kept half-looking and, when I saw he had missed, I jumped up and down like a lunatic and my friends turned to look at the pitch as the whistle went for full time.'

Sue Thornton was a 16-year-old Leeds supporter, attending - like myself - her first ever Wembley final. 'I had never been that far away from home before but I was allowed to go by my parents as my older brother was taking me. I wore a Leeds rugby jersey as a dress based on the players' kit before replica kits were available and had blue and amber ribbons in my hair. When Wakefield scored near the end of the game and it looked as though Don Fox would convert, I sat down almost in tears with my hands over my ears as I didn't want to hear the Wakefield fans cheering when the ball went over and they had won. I did hear cheering and suddenly my brother grabbed me by the collar, shouting, "He's missed. He's missed." I really was in tears then, but they were tears of joy as I saw the Leeds players celebrating.'

Another 16-year-old Leeds supporter, Ron Rosenhead, was also attending his first Wembley final and was seated by his father directly alongside the try-line at the Leeds end of the ground. 'When the final try was scored I looked at my father and he looked at me. Nothing was said. Not a word. Don Fox came to kick and I decided to look. Once he had, I couldn't understand why the Leeds players were jumping for joy. I turned to my father and asked him. Then there were shouts all round us. "He's missed it!" As we were exactly in line with the try-line, all you could see was one upright. There was no way we could see whether he'd kicked it or not and, to be honest, both of us forgot about the touch judges. We had no idea he did not kick the goal.'

Mel Reuben recalls that he and thousands of Leeds fans had launched into, 'Ee Aye Addio - We've Won the Cup' after Risman's penalty had taken the score to 11-7. Then came the Hirst try. 'We were shell-shocked. My mate had a huge Leeds rosette. He tore it off his coat, jumped on it, shouted a few choice swear words and promptly stood up and said, "I'm off." As Don Fox was lining up his kick, most of the Leeds fans were making their way to the exits, myself included. Suddenly, there was an almighty shout from the Leeds end as he missed the conversion. We turned round and saw the Leeds players jumping up in the air, running past a dejected Fox. My mate was on his hands and knees looking for his rosette as most of the Leeds fans streamed back into the stadium. I, and thousands of Loiners fans, never saw the Don Fox kick.'

Wakefield supporter George Denton, who had been standing at the match alongside Eric Timmins, 'Pud' Hemingway and Barry and Keith Lodge, remembers someone else on the floor as the match reached its incredible conclusion. 'Barry Lodge just collapsed in a heap, in shock. He just couldn't believe it. We had to pick him up.'

'The greatest of dramas are not scripted,' wrote Tim Wilkinson and Ray Gent many years later and the sensational final seconds are recorded in detail by Geoffrey Moorhouse in the game's official history. 'The Leeds players stood watching, in attitudes of exhaustion and numbness, as Fox very carefully placed the ball, stepped back five paces, paused for a moment before moving forward, and swung into his kick. As his boot made contact, the ball squirted like a piece of slippery soap past the right-hand upright, and the poor lad - as Eddie Waring informed the nation - went down on his knees to beat the treacherous earth in anguish and dismay.' It was, according to Robert Gate, 'the most famous missed goal of all time.' Reporting on the match in the following day's *Sunday Mirror*, Waring suggested that, 'Master of suspense Alfred Hitchcock couldn't have produced a more dramatic or sensational finish.'

Bev Risman stood by the posts as Fox lined up the conversion. 'I watched him kicking the goal. I'd never even dreamt that he would miss it. Those who've studied it say that his non-kicking foot slipped, he slid and didn't make contact so I'm quite prepared to accept that. I had a feeling that he tried to build a mound out of the water. As a result, when his foot slipped, he lost contact altogether.'

Barry Seabourne was one of the Leeds players who faced Fox as he was taking the kick. 'I watched it and couldn't believe it when he twanged it. I don't think he kicked for the conditions. We thought he was sure to do it but he'd mentally kicked the goal before he actually had. When it missed and he flopped on the floor, I felt for him.'

From the side of the posts, Ken Eyre was a close observer and has his own thoughts on what went wrong. 'To me, the ball seemed to be up too high. It was on its point instead of being down. Kickers in wet conditions always sunk the ball a bit deeper. Remember, then, they weren't using tees, it was a heel-in. It seemed to me as though he'd have been better putting it down lower, then more of his boot would have got the leather at the bottom of the ball. Instead of driving through it with his head down, his foot came across and that spins the ball off to the right. It spiralled outside the post.'

For Syd Hynes the scene is as clear to him now as it was then. 'The main thing I remember is when they did score that last try, me and Mick Shoebottom went right to the corner flag. We were looking at the crowd, saying to each other, "Shit. We've lost this in the last minute." And then the ball came trickling past us in the corner and we said, "Shit. Has he hit the post or something?" All the players nearer jumped up and we realised we'd held on and won.'

Ian Brooke shook his head in disbelief at the same time. 'It was that wet, the conditions and it just skidded off his boot. I'd say nine times out of ten - no, ten times out of ten - with Don, he'd kick it. His boots were - kind of - curled up at the front with the water. Everybody's were absolutely wet through and soaked and they were getting miss-shaped with the weather. That was a factor.' Peter Fox contrasts the boots he had worn while playing in the sixties with those his brother wore in that final. 'I had a solid pair of toes on mine. His were turned up and went to a point. How he got his foot to the ball I don't know.'

Trinity captain that day Harold Poynton has another view of what was behind rugby league's most famous missed kick. 'I think the pressure might have got to him a little bit. There's 90,000 people in and a last-minute crunch kick to win. I just thought it was nerves.' From the bench at the side of the pitch, Mick Morgan shared a similar sentiment. 'If it had been from the touchline, I think he might have kicked it. It seems a daft statement but I think it was that easy, he knew, and I think he was nervous. The nerves got to him.'

Alan Smith feels that a number of factors should be considered. 'You can talk about psychological pressure. It can happen in any sport, where someone will miss a simple shot at snooker or a penalty at football. You look at the conditions. It was still riddled with water. It was still floating with water. To kick a ball in that, he's to compose himself and can you imagine that toe-cap at the end of a point of a ball. All the best kickers missed easy ones. But if Don was going to miss one, the odds were stacked that day. Everything - conditions, the psychology, the pressure, the weather, the ball, the toe-end, everything - was stacked against him. And it was a sad carry-on for Don.' His son Greg recalls, 'He said to me that at that time it was Neil who was the obvious kicker and it was the expectation at the end of the match. It was, "Here Don. We've won it," sort of thing.'

Geoff Oakes with the Wakefield bench party had a somewhat different perspective on what went wrong. 'To be quite honest, I think he had his head up a bit. I think he was wanting to watch it go through, like you do at golf sometimes. Side-kickers would have got that easily. They wouldn't have sliced it.' Tony Crosby has a view that, perhaps, Fox wanted with his final kick to make a triumphalist point at the end of the game. 'Perhaps he thought "Well boys, this is it. I'm going to kick this over the stand and we're winning" and that's it.'

Fox's brothers, Peter and Neil, share the same, strongly

held, view that the Wakefield bench that day bear some responsibility for the goal miss. Peter Fox describes his thoughts at the time. 'Our Don picked the ball up. He looked at the ball which, as we know, was sodden. He looked at his shirt which must have been soaked and I knew what he was going to do. He was going to wipe the ball on his shirt. And I'm thinking, "why doesn't somebody from the Wakefield camp rush onto the field with a towel or something?"'

Looking back at this match at a time when, in current games, any number of support staff in bright T-shirts seem to be able to enter the arena during play it is, perhaps, important to reflect on whether the Wakefield bench could have intervened at this point. From his experience, both as a player and a coach, Peter Fox is in no doubt. 'Yes. They could have done. Nobody could have stopped them. I'd have done it as a coach, even let him wipe it on my shirt or jumper. I'd have raced onto the field because that's what I knew he was thinking about. He'd got to wipe the ball or dry the ball on something to get rid of the amount of moisture that was on it. He was just stood there looking.'

Neil Fox also believes it would have been permissible to send someone on from the sidelines to enable his brother to dry the ball. 'Don was trying to wipe the ball on his shirt. It was impossible because it was soaking wet. We've talked about it and Peter has said - like I have - why didn't Paddy Armour run onto the field with a towel?' He is of the view that this should have happened and could have happened. 'I think they would have had to ask permission. But the top and bottom of it was, when he did place that ball, the bottom two inches of it was in water. He's kicking at the bottom of the ball, he's hit the water in front of it and sliced the kick.'

Peter Fox also mentions the likely effect of surface water long before kicking tees were introduced in the game. 'He made his heel mark in the ground and the hole would have filled up with water immediately. He had to place the ball in water and stick it up somehow. How he did that was amazing, I couldn't see how he would.' Roger Ingham, viewing the conversion attempt from his seat near the front, vividly underlines Peter Fox's description of what happened. 'It was like trying to kick it out of a trench on a building site by that time,' he says.

A former player who had grown up with Don in Sharlston and been his half-back partner at Featherstone Rovers said that, if he had been Trinity's captain that day, he wouldn't have asked Don to take that final conversion. In an article entitled, 'Why I would never have let my great friend take that final kick' in the *Yorkshire Post* on 22 August, 2008, Joe Mullaney felt another player should have been given the crucial task because Fox was somewhat suspect taking kicks from what most would regard as the easiest position.

'Most of the goals Don kicked for Featherstone were from the right or left of the posts. It didn't matter how wide out the kick was, you could rely on Don to hit the target. Unfortunately, he was always a little bit unpredictable in front of the sticks. It would have been a big call but I know for certain I would have had the guts to say "Let someone else kick this one."'

David Jeanes says he never gave a thought about Fox not attempting the goal, but confirms Mullaney's point. 'A few weeks before then, the same thing - more or less - had happened at Bramley. We'd gone to play in one of these Easter games. We were playing three games in four days so you're absolutely knackered and, in a similar situation, Don missed a goal from a similar sort of place as well.'

At the end of eighty minutes, played in normal conditions, most players will be pretty tired. The conditions of Wembley '68, would have sapped the strength of the youngest and fittest players. At 32 years of age, Fox had played a central role in Trinity's performance that day both with his normal distributive skills and his crucial kicking game which had led to both Hirst tries. He was by then a veteran and interviewed nearly a week after the final, he'd said, 'It was the happiest moment of my career walking out on that pitch at Wembley. I'd had nearly every honour in the game and this [a Challenge Cup winner's medal] was the one I hadn't got after 14 years of rugby league.'

But, in addition, the former scrum-half, turned loose forward, was playing out of position in the front row at a time when rugby league had competitive scrums. Ken Eyre had propped against Don Fox in the scrum that day and adds another important point to the range of theories around the goal miss. 'He was a great footballer but he was not a number ten. Don had a torrid time in that pack, I'll tell you. When we go on about that particular incident - I have my thoughts - but I reckon one of the things is he was shattered.'

Fox's son, Greg, is dismissive of the idea that exhaustion played a part, saying his father never mentioned it as a factor. 'I've heard comments like that before and I've seen it, reading on the internet, "Why was Don Fox a prop in that match?" My dad had been a scrum-half. He'd been a very big scrum-half at five foot ten and a half. I think he was thirteen stone something when he was seventeen, so he was a well-set man. His main position was scrum-half or loose forward. But I think my dad had the ability and skill to pull any position off to be quite honest. And he was always - and he was renowned for it - an extremely strong bloke. Nobody could beat him at arm-wrestling. He was very strong but he certainly wasn't a prop.'

Up in his commentary position, Ken Rollin remembers

that after Hirst had scored the final try he told the commentator that Wakefield had won the match, threw his pen against the wall and went out of the room. He actually didn't see his old friend miss the conversion. 'At the end you could hear this terrific cheer. I didn't know who had won or lost. Then all I could see was Don coming back with his head down and I realised he'd missed it. The commentator gave me £20 and said, "You've done alright."'

John Atkinson says of the goal miss that he also never actually saw it live. 'I was laid down and I just couldn't believe that all this had happened in the last seconds. There was no time left. Even though Neil wasn't playing, Don's goal-kicking ability wasn't bad. And then I heard, I think it was Mick Shoebottom most of all, jumping up and down and I'm looking round wondering what had happened. "He's missed it," Bernard Watson said. "He's missed the goal." So I joined in.'

Not only did some of the Leeds players feel unable to watch the kick but, among the spectators, Doreen Clark, the wife of the skipper turned away as it was being taken. 'I just couldn't look,' she told the *Yorkshire Post* at the time, 'and neither could most of the other Leeds players' wives who were present.'

Ken Eyre suggests that he was probably the first player to react because Fox's kick had gone to the outside of the goalpost he was leaning on. 'I was up in the air because I knew there was a cup-winner's medal coming.' Alan Smith adds, 'The feelings? It was wow! I was a cup winner. It didn't matter whether this was a try or that was a try or the goal missed. It was hard lines. That's how sport is.' Albert Eyre had other considerations, 'When he missed it, I realised we'd got winning money. I think it was £120, which was a lot in those days. And I think we got £10 from the Milk Marketing Board.'

They Walked on Water

Eyre's recollection of a sponsorship deal involving milk involves one of the more bizarre incidents in a match full of rather odd occurrences. Among the possessions of Tony Capstick, a collector of rugby league memorabilia, is a letter from the National Milk Council which belonged to Trinity's coach Ken Traill, outlining an agreement to pay £100 into the players' fund on the basis that they would be seen, if they won, drinking milk after the match. Eyre says, 'Apparently the crates were in the corridor and they moved them into the Wakefield dressing room when they scored and then - the story we heard - they brought them back into ours.'

The agreement with the National Milk Council had been made with both sides, with the payment being made just to the winners. It included a requirement that, during the week before the final the players had to be photographed, 'associating milk with their training,' according to the letter dated 7th May, 1968, from M.A. Esten, Public Relations and Promotions, National Milk Council. It was also arranged that a toast should be drunk in milk in the winning dressing room. In addition, the schedule included a payment of £25 to the winning captain if he drank a bottle of milk on the Wembley pitch.

If the winning players were jubilant over the amount they would receive for winning, the financial consequences of Fox's miss for the Wakefield team obviously added to his personal despair. Ken Traill didn't exactly beat about the bush in comments which were reported on the Monday after the final in the *Daily Express*. 'Oooh, the money, the money that's been lost,' he is reported as saying in an article which analysed exactly what defeat had cost his side. While the National Milk Council payment of £125 was not mentioned in the piece, it suggested, 'That missed kick had cost Trinity's team £3,500 made up of a bet of £200 at 10-1 at the start of the season that they would win the Cup and £100 a man bonus.'

Mick Morgan's recollection is that the Trinity players stood to earn around £350 each - 'a small fortune' - and the amount was made up of the match payments and the winnings from the bet. 'All the directors had clubbed together and put a bet on, at whatever odds there were, and obviously that was going to be shared between the players. So it was a lot of money.'

Traill added to his remarks on the monetary implications with criticism of Fox's approach to that final kick and a prediction of what his failure would mean for him in later life. 'But it's not that [the lost money] alone, it's the pride and the honour, all lost. It's historic, this. They'll point at him in 20 years and say, remember. He's got to live with it. I'm sorry for him, but I'll say this, I think he didn't concentrate, he was too casual.'

Tony Hannan suggests that re-running the black and white pictures of those last few seconds now, '…can feel like intruding on personal grief' and Harry Jepson recalls that there was, ever after, among those who knew Don, a reluctance to talk to him about what happened that day. 'Those of us who are interested in the game as a whole, we never spoke about it to him. Maybe we should have - I don't know - but we all felt sympathy towards him because it was such a terrible thing to happen, not just because it was in front of 90,000 people, but its impact went world-wide.'

He was right about the goal miss being something of a taboo subject but, many years later, at another Wembley final, I had a detailed conversation with Don about the circumstances surrounding the end of that match. I had known him some years by that time but had never broached the subject of the missed kick, knowing the impact that painful episode had had on his subsequent life. But I had introduced him to Roger Stott, at that time the Member of

They Walked on Water

Parliament for Wigan, and, once the penny had dropped as to which Fox this was, Roger had typically gone straight in with a question about the incident. Don very much echoed his brother Peter's take on what happened, with reference to the state of the pitch and particularly the ball. But he talked also about the sodden state of his boots that day and, in a comment I had not seen noted anywhere previously, made a particular point about the impact of the cotton wool packing his boot toe-cap which had also become sodden.

It was some time after this discussion that I came across an interview with Don in the magazine *Total Sport* in which he spoke in detail about his memory of the goal miss. He put the incident in the full context of the particular pressure on him at the time and again referred specifically to the state of the cotton wool in his boot. As part of a series called, 'Not Your Night Son. Personal Disasters' recalled,' he is quoted as saying, 'When I went up to take the kick, I could really feel the pressure. We'd won the League the week before so I knew that I was kicking for the double as well as the Cup and that made me very nervous. But I honestly did think I'd kick it. After all, I'd already kicked two really good goals, one from forty yards and one from the touchline, earlier in the game and this one was right in front of the posts. It was like a little putt. But I've seen these top golfers miss what you'd think were dead easy putts and that's what happened to me. I lined it up but, when I hit it, it just sliced off the side of my boot and sailed past the post. I'd put cotton wool in my boots because I was taking the kicks which I didn't normally do. It was so wet the cotton wool had gone soggy. I don't know if that had anything to do with it. When I'd missed I could feel everyone staring at me and when I were going up to collect my medal I could see all these little kids crying and that really broke my heart. I remember thinking "Bloody 'ell, look what I've caused."'

Greg Fox says his father rarely commented on the incident but he recalled at one point asking, '"Look, dad. Did you bottle it or something?" He never really talked about it, but he said, "no."' His father did, however, speak to him about the issue of the state of his boots and the implications, perhaps, of his failure to change them at half-time. 'He kept his boots on at half-time. The pitch was so waterlogged and they got saturated. But being a bit superstitious, he kept them on, thinking "I've done two kicks, one from the touchline." What had happened is the toe-cap had warped so it had turned up. As he came to kick the ball it actually hit the underside of the sole and those days they used a old leather ball.'

Mick Morgan, who had signed for Trinity as a 16-year-old and been driven to training from his home in Featherstone by Don Fox, his boyhood hero as a Rovers player, remembers one particular remark he made after the final indicating his concern over the implications of the Wembley miss for his son, Greg. 'He said to me - I can't remember whether it was at Wembley or back in Featherstone - "My young 'un'll be fighting over that at school." I think it preyed a lot on his mind.'

David Lawrenson has recorded that Eddie Waring's, 'He's a poor lad' comment featured in the *Times* newspaper's list of 25 favourite sporting quotes during 2006, while Tony Hannan made the point that, 'Soccer has Kenneth Wolstenholme's "they think it's all over": rugby league has Eddie Waring's "poor lad".' The commentator's nephew, Harry Waring, explains that the context of these remarks that day have, perhaps, never been fully appreciated. Some years earlier, on the 1962 Great Britain tour of Australia, his only trip Down Under, Fox had got to know Eddie Waring who was one of a number of media representatives travelling with the team. 'When Don Fox was injured after playing in only five games and was having to be repatriated home because of it, Eddie had a lot of sympathy for him. He and one or two of the other journalists approached the management to persuade them to release Don from the tour so that he could have a little holiday up the Gold Coast. They gave permission and Eddie and some others put their hands in their pockets.'

Fox's misfortune eight years earlier probably hadn't been forgotten by Eddie. As Harry Waring points out, 'This was Don's first Cup final. He'd already played in four previous semi-finals, losing them all - three for Featherstone and one for Wakefield - and, as a 32-year-old, he was getting towards the end of his career. So Eddie had all the sympathy for this chap or 'lad' as he would call him. When Wakefield scored the try in the last minute, in a game which should probably never have been played, Eddie went straightaway for the human angle and said the first thing that came into his head which was, "The poor lad…"'

Peter Fox sums up his thoughts viewing that television clip.'Eddie Waring said, "He's missed it! He's missed it!" And then our Don fell onto his knees with his head in his hands, because he knew what he'd done, or rather what he hadn't done. Then, Eddie Waring saw the magic of the moment and said, "Poor lad". He grasped, at the vital moment, the situation and the trauma. He realised what a terrible shame it was for our Don to have missed the goal.' As Harry Waring notes, the way his uncle captured that moment will probably never be forgotten. 'The phrase catapulted both Don and Eddie into international stardom. The BBC tapes of that particular incident went round the world and are still played to this day.'

Chapter Fourteen

After the whistle blew

It comes over very clearly, in discussions with the Leeds players who were out there that day, that there was no real triumphalism at the end of the game and a very real feeling of empathy towards Don Fox. John Atkinson remarks about the fact that, in particular, there were no humorous cracks or sarcastic comments in his direction in the immediate aftermath of his goal miss. 'What I do remember is that Don was on the floor and as the Leeds lads went past him, not one said anything derogatory to him, "Well done!" or anything like that, just, "Don. Hard lines." There was always something special about rugby in those days. You sympathised, he'd missed a goal in front of the posts to win the rugby league cup. I think we all knew the repercussions for him from it.'

Perhaps, because this final had been played in such appalling conditions, it was inevitable that mistakes would play a huge part in the eventual outcome and there was a feeling among the Leeds players that, 'There, but for the grace of God...' Bernard Watson's failure to trap Fox's last kick-off could have lost them the game and Atkinson was conscious that his role in respect of the first Ken Hirst try could also have been crucial. 'It would have been the same for me if it had been the last try of the match when I'd knocked it back, Kenny had scored and they'd have won the match. I'd have had that to live with.'

'I knew,' continues Atkinson, 'that this was the worst place, the last minute of the match, the winning kick and everything, for it to happen.' The Leeds players were, he maintains, 'very, very sympathetic to him because, apart from the fact he was a good lad - a smashing bloke - we were all professional rugby players. It could have happened to us all.'

John Atkinson has clearly given a great deal of thought to Fox's situation that day and says that what happened as the Leeds players walked past him, always sticks in his mind. 'In modern day football, if you'd missed the last penalty to win the FA Cup - it goes over the top, miles away - all the team would have been taking the mickey out of you like nobody's business. Fox was on the floor. We could see the state he was in.'

While Fox's desolation at the end of that game was understandable, Atkinson's recollections of coming off the field may give some clue as to why some of the Leeds player's reactions were not what might have been expected from Wembley winners. Bev Risman, for example, clearly had very mixed feelings. 'I was absolutely ecstatic, but then I thought how can we win a cup like this? We were the winners but for it all to end like that with Wakefield having the chance of taking it from us when we'd got it won, emotions were in turmoil really.' Ken Rollin describes how, having come down from his commentary position, he entered the Leeds dressing room perhaps three-quarters of an hour after the match had ended when the players were changed. 'As I walked in and said, "Fantastic," somebody said to me: "We didn't win that. Wakefield lost it." That's how it was. And of course, everybody at that stage was thinking about Don. In actual fact, he'd won the match and lost it within thirty seconds.'

Ian Brooke clearly remembers his feelings as the final whistle blew. 'Sad, very sad. Sad for Don, sad because we didn't like losing to Leeds. We used to have some really great games with Leeds. But ultimately, you just felt sorry for Don because all the pressure then had been put on him.'

For Risman there were concerns, as well, over how his wife Ann was coping with the incredible drama as a spectator at the match. She was expecting their third child and was three weeks overdue at the time of the final. 'The question was, is she going to come and, of course, being Ann, she was. But we were hoping that the baby might have come beforehand. She took her chaperone with her and her doctor so there was somebody there if something happened. I immediately thought at that time, "What's Ann thinking about now after all that stuff?" That went through my mind on the field.' As it turned out, he was in Australia, as captain of the World Cup team, when at 5.00 a.m. on the morning of the opening game, he received a phone call notifying him of the birth of his third son.

Barry Seabourne remembers that after the match Leeds players had gone into the Wakefield dressing room. 'I just went in to commiserate. I was a big friend of Ken Traill, who was a pal of my dad's. There was not a right lot we could say but we shook hands.' Back in the Leeds dressing room, Risman recalled that Mick Clark, the Leeds captain, made clear his view that no-one had deserved to lose in those circumstances. But with the Cup on the table and the winners medals received, there were, nevertheless, understandable celebrations. Ken Eyre says, 'We were euphoric and we were shattered, running in that. I know that little Arthur Crowther [the kit man] pulled my shirt off and I'd dye run onto my body. Nobody was jumping about, but obviously we were pleased. We'd won the Cup.'

Tony Crosby particularly remembers how clean all the shirts were at the end of the game because of the soaking conditions it had been played in throughout. 'We came off after the match and we could have taken that shirt off, folded it, taken it home and dried it because there was no mud. It was unbelievable.' Like all the other players, he was exhausted and recalls the relief of lying in one of the single baths in the dressing room. 'I had damaged ribs, although I didn't realise at the time. Matt McLeod just caught me with his knees in the last ten minutes, so I was just relaxing in the warm water.'

In the Wakefield dressing room, Ian Brooke says the players, 'were all just sat there really sloughed, just thinking to ourselves, "we've got robbed" because we felt we were the better side. Everybody's played well under difficult circumstances, nobody's let you down, everybody's played their part - and we didn't feel that Don had because he was a great footballer. Nobody, to my knowledge, in that dressing room said to Don, when he came in, "You lost us the match" or owt like that. Everyone was great with him, supportive to him. I don't think anybody ever said that. To be honest, if anybody had they'd have got a real...from all the team. Nobody mentioned it because you know how fallible you are yourself. We all make mistakes. The one thing we always had in a Wakefield dressing was harmony and a togetherness. I think that proved the point that day.'

Harold Poynton recalls: 'We were gutted. There were no hard feelings against Leeds. We were sick but you take it as it goes. Only two weeks before that we'd slaughtered them at Belle Vue. We couldn't blame Don, he'd had a marvellous game.' Poynton's half-back partner, Ray Owen, apparently told Fox, 'If it hadn't been for you we would never have been in a position to win' according to the *Daily Express*.

David Jeanes strongly reinforces this point. 'We all stuck together. I always thought that one of the main differences between rugby union and rugby league was that rugby union players stuck together, rugby league players didn't. But we did. Everybody was friends. No enemies and we all kept together.' But, within the Wakefield dressing room after the game he notes,'There was a, sort of, deadly silence. I can't remember at what stage his brother Neil came in to talk to Don. Don wasn't speaking to anybody. He was basically sat there - as far as I remember - not wanting to talk. People came knocking on the door, wanting to come in but no-one wanted to have a conversation with anybody really. We were just saying, "come on, let's get away from here. We don't want to be hanging about."'

The interview that BBC's David Coleman undertook with Don Fox at the end of the game may not have seen as many replays as the infamous goal miss but it is surely just as iconic. It was highlighted many years later, on the occasion of Coleman's 70th birthday, to commemorate his noted 'malapropism-at-a-magic-moment,' according to Jim White in his piece, 'And Coleman is 70…quite remarkable…' in *The Independent*, on 26th April, 1996. Such things were the basis of 'Colemanballs', the long-running, celebrated column in *Private Eye*. White charts the interaction. 'Fox's torment…was not complete. Waiting in the wings with a microphone to interview him as he stumbled off the pitch was the dapper figure of David Coleman. "Don, it must be a desperate thing for a situation like that to occur," said Coleman, the much-mimicked voice eager with anticipation. "Shocking," replied

Fox, his eyes dead with pain. "I'm that upset I can't speak." "Anyway," said Coleman, brushing away such trivial concerns, "I've got some tremendous news, I know you don't know. You've been awarded the Lance Todd Memorial Trophy for outstanding contribution on the field of play. That must be some consolation, surely?"' White wrote of the Fox interview that, 'All the ingredients are there of a typical Coleman moment. Enthusiasm, the keen eye for detail and a passion for delivering news, all leavened by an ability to put his foot so far in it, he's up to the hairline. The kind of stuff, in short, that has made David Coleman a national institution, the inspiration behind the finest-ever *Spitting Image* sketch, in which the puppet Coleman, finger raised to hold his ear-piece, gets somewhat over-excited during a commentary: "Er, er, and I've gone far, far too early," splutters the puppet. "It will be impossible to keep up this level of excitement without my head exploding."' Which, as White notes, it does.

White is correct in noting that what we see on television is Fox telling Coleman that the Lance Todd award doesn't make up for the fact that Trinity lost the match. It has, however, been suggested that this was a re-recorded, polite version of Fox's initial responses to the interviewer's crass insensitivity in the circumstances. John Atkinson says that, as he was leaving the field, Coleman had said to Fox, '"Well. Really sorry about this but - if it's a consolation - you've won the Lance Todd Trophy." I think Don said something like, "Well, I'm not effing bothered about that." I know he was rude, because I was very close to him when he said it.'

Graham Chalkley, who along with his brothers Gordon and Barry, had grown up in Sharlston and were friends of Fox, confirms there was an earlier filmed episode of this interview. Recorded in Robert Light's book, when initially told by Coleman that he had won the Lance Todd, Fox apparently retorted, 'Stick it up thi arse,' saying 'I don't want it.' Trinity's Ian Brooke confirms Chalkley's story. 'We were sat in the dressing room and somebody - Paddy Armour, I think - came in and said, "You'll never guess what Don's said to Coleman." I says "What?" and Paddy said, "He's told him to shove it [the Lance Todd Trophy] up his arse!" We all fell about laughing. I said "He hasn't, has he? What on live TV?" He says "Aye, yes." I said "Oh, they'll cut that out then."'

Don Fox's son Greg can back up the exchange with Coleman. 'I think he [Coleman] said something about the Lance Todd and my Dad said, basically, I'm not bothered because they'd just lost the match and he felt, obviously, that he's the one who's let the side down. They must have taped something again, the official version. Because I do remember my dad saying he told him where to put it.' Neil Fox feels his brother's reaction at the time was understandable. 'Don was not very happy. He'd got a losing medal. It wasn't just for himself he was saying it. It was because of the players he played with.'

Among Coleman's other post-match interviews that day was one with John Hebblethwaite, the match referee. It appears he got short shrift here as well. Hebblethwaite's son, David, recalls that he said to his father, '"Don't you think you gifted it to Leeds?" My dad just turned round and said "I wasn't kicking the goals for Wakefield" and that was it. He just walked past Coleman as though to say, "Get out of my way."'

Not long after Hebblethwaite was putting Coleman in his place that day, the referee's two sons, David, and his older brother Peter, were doing their best to keep dry as they came away from the match. David remembers, 'We were coming out of the stadium. It was still raining and my brother and I were in the queue and a [mounted] police officer came down and said, "Get back in the queue" because he'd moved onto the road to get away from this spout of water that was coming down. My brother said, "No. I'm not getting back under there." The officer gave the horse a dig with his spurs and it kicked Peter on the shin and nearly broke his leg!'

Coming away from the ground it was very easy to spot those spectators who had been in the better seats nearer to the front. Geoff Lee recalls coming down the steps after the game was over and seeing the woman who had been occupying 'his' seat and obviously enjoyed informing him that his ticket was invalid. 'She and all the group she was with were absolutely drenched!'

Schoolteacher Brian Robinson stayed with his Rothwell pupils for the Cup presentation, allowing the crowd to clear before taking his party back to their coach. 'During this time,' he says, 'a large, forlorn looking man was pacing up and down the terraces. It was Jack Wilkinson [the former Trinity and Great Britain prop], almost in tears, wishing all sorts of evil on the referee who had awarded the penalty try and offering to commit any atrocity on him so that justice could be done. To say he was upset would be the understatement of the century.' Robinson remembers something else that particularly struck him as he and the Rothwell boys were leaving the venue. 'As we left the ground the sun was shining and I looked back to see the ground staff with hosepipes watering the area behind the posts. Unbelievable!'

Roger Ingham also clearly recalls what was happening as he exited. 'The fans were arguing about this controversial incident [the obstruction try] as they came out. There were guys arguing and wringing their shirts out.'

While, there was inevitably some argument about the 68th minute incident, it is genuinely hard to put into words what was going round in the heads of supporters of both sides after that amazing match. In fact, it wasn't so much a match as an incredible, unforgettable experience and it took a long time for those who were there to fully come to terms with what collectively we had witnessed. It needed to be discussed, to be run and re-run in the mind and shared with others who were there, to be fully taken on board and understood. Most matches contain the odd incident which will be mulled over perhaps for the following week. This one had enough controversial content to last - as indeed it has done - a lifetime.

Like all Trinity supporters there that day, I went away feeling robbed by a refereeing decision. It wasn't the decision to play the match or continue it during impossible weather conditions. The state of the pitch was a factor faced by both sides and most fans of either side and the neutrals present had been glad that it had gone ahead, having undertaken, in most instances, a 400-mile round trip to see it. But the award of an obstruction try left those of us in the red, white and blue frankly feeling cheated out of what would have been the first Cup and League double in Trinity's history.

Perhaps it was that feeling of somehow being robbed which led to many of us who were there not taking in the full impact of the last-second goal miss in terms of its obvious effect on the result and on the player involved and his team-mates. We were at the opposite end of the field to the final try and conversion attempt so were too far away to really appreciate those tragic scenes of Fox on one knee after the miss which have been replayed so very often on our television screens. We were all confused, bemused and left. It's as simple as that.

Trinity's historian, John Lindley, summed up the end of that game so very accurately in his *Challenge for the Championship* brochure the following season. 'There were no prolonged cheers to announce the end of this game; everyone, victor and vanquished alike, were too stunned to express any such demonstrations.' Lindley suggested that for the Leeds side, '…it was almost as disappointing as for Wakefield; the only difference for them was their hold on the trophy. Unfortunately, through no fault of their own, success brought little of the joyous satisfaction and unstinted acclaim which winners should enjoy. It was indeed a tragic end to a final which had held a firmer place for luck and misfortune than for true football skills.'

I don't recall seeing Leeds collect the trophy and do the traditional lap of honour or seeing Fox comforted as he left the field, captured in the famous photograph with Matt McLeod and Gerry Round. Harry Edgar, editor of the *Rugby League Journal,* recalls the poignancy of that vivid image of McLeod putting his arm around Fox to console him. Edgar, a Cumbrian, knew Matt McLeod from his Whitehaven days and recalled that, 'he was the type of guy who would be so caring for a team-mate in distress, at a time when others maybe were more angry or disappointed for themselves at seeing victory dashed so cruelly by somebody's unfortunate mistake. Matt was such a laid-back fellow, who would take the loss in his stride, and just be grateful to have had the chance to play at Wembley.'

Harry Jepson sums up his feelings at the end of the game. 'The whistle was blown for time and everyone walked out of the ground in a sort of daze because they weren't quite sure what they'd seen. It was one of the most curious games of rugby league ever played which ended in the oddest way, and a terrible one for Wakefield and for the player concerned, but it was all in pattern with the game. It was an incredible afternoon.'

Chapter Fifteen

Celebrations and commiserations

Ian Brooke remarks that, if there had been celebrations in the Leeds camp immediately after the match, they were not particularly noisy. 'Their dressing room was the other side of the walkway but when we came out to go back on the bus, there was no singing or shouting. Nobody ever gloated or anything like that because I think they felt they were lucky and you don't take advantage of that. You're sportsmen and you take it in the true sportsmanlike manner that you should.'

After being defeated in such circumstances all the Trinity team were, understandably, deeply disappointed. Neil Fox, in particular, felt it was important the team stayed together at this point. 'After the game, the lads jumped on the bus to go back to the hotel. They were all upset, obviously, and Don was down. I just went round the lads and said, "When we get to the hotel, don't go straight to your rooms. We're going out for a drink with Don." And we all to the pub across the road.' Geoff Oakes describes the feelings in the

Trinity dressing room after the match. 'Obviously we were all down but the big thing was for Don. Everybody just wanted to get to the nearest pub and drown our sorrows. We all stuck together and that's exactly what we did. We went to the nearest pub, stopped there and got drunk!'

After the match, the Trinity team returned to Baileys Hotel in Kensington and Mick Morgan recalls Don Fox being approached by a reporter on the hotel steps. 'I remember Ken Trail coming out and turning him away.' Ian Brooke says they were all determined to support Fox after what he had gone through at the end of the game. 'We all said to Don, "Come on." Straight off the bus, straight into the Stanhope, got the beers in, all sat round the table, made sure he was with us, he was part of us. It wasn't his fault. We made him feel that we were with him. We regarded him still as a mate. He'd done nothing wrong to us. It could have happened to anybody.' David Jeanes recalls those discussions in the pub. 'Everyone was trying to get him out of his depression and saying, "We've got there, Don. We won a bloody cup the week before. It's not your fault that this happened."'

The players met up with their wives and girlfriends when they returned to Baileys for dinner. They had stayed at another hotel the previous night. Neil Fox recalls their reaction as they were reunited with their menfolk. 'Obviously, when the wives arrived, they were all upset. My wife Molly was upset for Don and said to him, "Don't worry. We'll get over it." We'd had a few jars by then and he seemed alright.'

Harry Jepson, a future employee with Leeds in various guises up to President, was also present at Bailey's. His Hunslet team had stayed there when they played at Wembley in 1965, having beaten Trinity in the semi-final. At the time, he was very friendly with Trinity committee man and former player Brian Briggs, who had invited him to come to Bailey's for a drink after the game. 'I said no, I won't be coming because, if you win, - and I wanted them to win, because all Hunslet people wanted them to beat Leeds - I don't want to see you after the game, but I will come down if you lose because there'll be nobody there except me and my wife. That's the arrangement I stuck to and we were the only people there.'

The Trinity players were drowning their sorrows across the road when he arrived and Jepson found himself in the company of the coaching staff and club committee. He remembers their reaction to the defeat. 'There was an air of, not despondency, but disappointment. Ken Traill, who was a very good friend of mine at that time, didn't have anything to say. Briggsy had plenty to say as he always had! John Ridge was very dejected indeed but, as far as I can remember, nobody mentioned the game.' According to Ridge himself, he had actually been in tears at one point at the hotel after the match. 'I was so frustrated,' he told the *Yorkshire Post*, referring to the awarding of the penalty try to Leeds.

From the players' perspective, Ian Brooke has much more positive memories of the occasion. 'You can ask anyone who was there in'68, but that was the best night we ever had. Honestly. Even when we'd won - I'd been there in '63, Harold and Neil in '60 and '62 - but that was the best after-dinner we'd ever had.' Speaking to those who were there that night, the impression is gained that, whereas the 1960 and 1962 Trinity sides split into different cliques in terms of closeness and friendships, the 1968 squad very much gelled as a group and that was particularly apparent that evening.

The speeches were short, Brooke remembers. 'Everybody was "Come on lads. Let's just enjoy it." I can't just put it into words how we felt about it all, but it was really good. We couldn't believe we'd lost and I've never enjoyed myself so much in losing. It was an unbelievable feeling because, in our hearts, we knew we hadn't lost. We knew we'd played the best that we could and we thought we were the better side.'

Geoff Oakes' wife Margaret, confirms Brooke's recollection of the evening. 'At the meal afterwards, when we were all together, we laughed more that night than in 1960 when we'd won it easily. Then, we were, sort of, in anti-climax shock that we'd won. Now we'd lost but the atmosphere was better. By the time we got back for the banquet we'd all had a few drinks. I don't think anyone wanted to show the sadness and disappointment, so it was a really good night.'

What isn't generally known is that Wakefield Trinity had planned in some detail in advance that the meal in Bailey's would be a formal banquet to celebrate the club winning the double. Barnsley-based Trinity supporter, Geoff Wake, is the proud possessor of an eight page souvenir menu produced for the banquet which he rescued from waste bins at the club's Belle Vue ground some time after the match. The menu's front page quite clearly states that the 'Official Banquet' was 'to honour the club on winning the 1967/8 R.L. Championship and the 1968 R.L. Cup - The Double'. Included in the publication were details of the club's patrons, committee and officials as well as honorary officers. It listed previous honours, Cup winning teams and Lance Todd Trophy winners and had features on the club's President, Alderman Frank West, Chairman John Ridge, captain Harold Poynton and coach, Ken Traill. It also included the names of all forty players who had featured in Trinity's first team during the 1967/68 season, along with training staff. The menu started with prawn cocktail followed by *vol au vent* of ham. The main meal consisted of roast saddle of lamb, *croquette* potatoes, minted garden peas and broccoli spears. The sweet was fruit salad with cream, followed by a cheese board and coffee.

The Leeds team and officials were booked into London's Park Lane Hotel for the night of the final where they were to be joined for the post-match banquet by their wives and girlfriends who had travelled down by coach on the Friday and stayed in separate accommodation. Syd Hynes says Leeds always treated the team well on issues such as accommodation. 'The Leeds club were so good at organising things like that. It was always the best where we stopped.'

It may have been the best but, according to Barry Seabourne, the players were more than a little shocked when putting their hands in their pockets to pay for a round. 'We went upstairs. It was amazing what it cost for a drink. I used to have orange and lemonade. I didn't like beer. The prices were incredible. We couldn't believe it. We thought we were buying the bloody hotel when we were buying a drink!'

John Atkinson is unlikely to forget his overnight stay in what he describes as, 'the poshest hotel I've ever been in, in my life.' He retains very clear memories of the reactions of other guests to the arrival of the Leeds party. 'We were out of our depth really. You'd got these lads from all over the north of England, all going into the Park Lane Hotel and you could see people looking. And all these girls with scarves on, rattles and things. You could see people in the Park Lane Hotel thinking "What the hell?"'

Tony Crosby was to leave his mark at the hotel during his one and only stay there. 'I remember leaving the shower curtain outside the bath and wetting the floor which was carpeted. By mistake I left the curtain out and, when I stepped out, that carpet was absolutely soaked.' Kath, his wife remembers 'It was like the Wembley turf. It was absolutely sodden!'

Among those with the Leeds party was Arthur Clues, the larger than life Australian, who had given distinguished service to both the Leeds and Hunslet clubs in the 1940s and 1950s, and gone on to run a very successful sports shop in the centre of Leeds following his retirement as a player. Atkinson relates what happened. 'We're going to book in and Cluesy's there as I'm walking in. I got the room key and I'm going upstairs with Carol, who became my first wife. He shouts at the top of his voice in his Australian accent - it's full of people, this hotel, and you can appreciate, they were all well to do - "Going upstairs for an effin' jump, Atki?" I thought, oh no!'

Ken Eyre has a memory of most of the players going for a drink at what he describes as, 'a pub round the corner.' Atkinson is a bit more specific. 'Roy Francis said, before we had the meal, 'Come on.' And he took us to the Hilton, round the back, for a drink.' It seems, according to Atkinson, that the reaction to the arrival of the Leeds lads there was not dissimilar to that when they had entered the Park Lane. 'Again, you could see people looking, thinking "Who's this load of vagabonds coming in here?" Roy bought a round of drinks which came to about twenty quid. We said, "How much? Twenty quid?" I mean we were on £100 to win the match and he'd bought this round for twenty quid. You'd no chance of getting that in a week at work then. We were all talking about it. "He's spent twenty quid on this round of drinks." And I think one of the forwards said, "Well, he'll probably claim it back off the club." Knowing Roy, he probably did!'

Later in the evening, the Leeds entourage were invited to a cocktail party at 8.00 p.m. in a room on the ground floor of the Park Lane Hotel, adjacent to the Banqueting Hall where, at 8.30 p.m., they sat down to a celebratory five course dinner. It is open to question if many of the players knew exactly what they were in for from a perusal of the menu. After *Hors d'Oeuvre Riches, Supreme de Sole Breval* was served. The main meal was *Caneton d'Aylesbury Bigarrade, Petit Pois Fins a l'Etuvee* and *Pommes Dorees*. The sweet - *Souffle Alaska* and *Certise Jubile* - was followed by *Petit Fours* and coffee. The accompanying wines were *Pouilly-Fuisse*, 1964, *Beaune*, 1962 and *Moet & Chandon Dry Imperial*. A toast was proposed to the Leeds club by Col. Lawrence Turnbull, the Lord Mayor of Leeds who, according to the *Yorkshire Post*, 'recalled the part played by the late Sir Edwin Airey in making Headingley 'the greatest international centre of cricket and football." In his response the club chairman Alfred Sharman said, 'This is the best Leeds side we have ever had,' adding that, 'success has been achieved by a massive exercise.' The Leeds Football Committee chairman Jack Myerscough also spoke, along with the team captain, Mick Clark.

Of the evening Bev Risman says, 'The thing I remember most of all it that Roy Francis didn't take any part in anything to do with it. He was, believe it or not, a very emotional man, very tied up with his thoughts - a fantastic psychologist. He obviously had thoughts about how we shouldn't have won the match like this. It would have been so great if we'd won it like we beat Wigan in the semi-final, with wonderful rugby.' Alan Smith also came away with something of a sense of anti-climax. 'The whole experience - from falling on my backside, my involvement in the game was nil, everybody was sliding about and that was a disappointment really. I didn't want my first appearance at Wembley to be like that.'

Albert Eyre remembers the evening well. 'It was very nice. Everyone was on a high, and Leeds looked after you.

They Walked on Water

They looked after the wives and everything. We had a lovely reception. Everybody got a bit pie-eyed, it was like winning the bloody Lottery! We walked into our bedroom - me and the wife - and went, "Bloody hell fire!" It was just like being a film star, a celebrity. Everybody came away with writing pads and Park Lane Hotel pens and that.'

Alan Smith recalls thinking, 'This is posh stuff. This is really big stuff. It was another world.' He gives the impression, however, that most of the Leeds squad would perhaps have preferred to be elsewhere that evening. 'The Park Lane experience was fine with the grandeur and the surroundings - something we'd never experienced. But we wanted to relax and it wasn't what we were used to. We tried to get out from Park Lane to where there was some activity on. I remember trying to get a taxi on Park Lane and we couldn't. We just stayed in the bar and went to bed. It really fizzled out.'

Chapter Sixteen

On the way home

In view of the controversies surrounding this match there might have been an expectation of some trouble between the respective fans in the aftermath but rugby league's reputation for the generally good behaviour of the sport's followers was very much maintained by those present at Wembley in 1968.

David Atkinson recalls being particularly struck by the harmonious relationship between both sets of supporters at the end of an incredible game. 'As we left there was obviously tremendous disappointment. However there was no chanting by the Leeds supporters, no recriminations by the Wakefield spectators and everyone was simply discussing the game in the spirit of the sport.'

Following the match our group of around a dozen broke up as some chose to head for home almost straightaway. One of them was a traumatised Mick Slater. 'You were that young to have the sadness because, when I watched Wakefield in those days, it was the be all and end all. I used to feel it in my stomach if I couldn't get to the

161

match. It was an occasion, it was the meeting point was Trinity. So after the match - devastated - we were all going to go into London.' But Slater, who had not long before got married at the age of nineteen and now had a young baby, was determined to return home immediately and, along with Ian Taylor, caught a train at Wembley Park station which took him all the way back to Wakefield.

Bob Harrison remembers that the remaining members of our group travelled back to Leicester Square. He gives a good illustration of the fact that some of us were still very much growing up. 'We bought some badges from a bloke with a mobile stall. The badges we bought just said "F.O." and you clipped them behind your lapel. If you were confronted you just pulled your lapel back to reveal the badge. I think it was cool at the time!'

I have absolutely no memory of the journey to Wakefield on the train and suspect that most of the gang I was with, having not been to bed since Thursday night and sampled more beers in the West End after the match, dozed or slept much of the way back. Like David Atkinson, my recollection of the post-match atmosphere is one of genuinely friendly banter between both sets of fans despite the contentious issues surrounding the match. Indeed, just a couple of weeks after the final, the *Wakefield Express* reported that Trinity's Secretary-Manager, Eddie Thomas, had received, 'a glowing tribute to the exemplary conduct of Wakefield Trinity supporters who visited Wembley for the Challenge Cup final.' Thomas had been sent a letter, containing an extract from a report by the station master at Kings Cross Underground station, saying, 'In these days when football crowds receive much adverse publicity, it becomes a pleasant duty to report to you on the splendid behaviour of the supporters of the Rugby League Cup finalists, May 11. Everywhere they went they left behind them a feeling of goodwill due to their excellent conduct.' Noting that Kings Cross staff had been in a position to judge them from their arrival until the last departures on the 1.00 a.m. train the following morning, the letter asked, 'Would you be kind enough to convey our sincere thanks to the visitors from Leeds and Wakefield who set a good example to all football supporters everywhere?'

It is a matter of opinion how good an example the folk I was with set that night but, in accordance with what we were told was cup weekend tradition, we ended the Saturday evening in a Soho strip club. Goodness knows what the strippers thought as they disrobed to a constant barrage of coarse northern banter, ribald comment and wit. As one girl ended her performance with the removal of her G-string, I noticed my mate Bob Harrison sound asleep with his mouth wide open.

Eric Timmins, Eric 'Pud' Hemingway and Barry and Keith Lodge had planned to celebrate in London with a few more beers before returning north. However, Timmins says, 'None of us could face another pint as we all felt sick at the events of the game so where could we go to pass on a few hours? Let's head to Soho. We'd never been there. Would you believe it, early Saturday evening and we found ourselves in a strip club with an audience of only ten including us four lads sat on the front row for a good view. The first stripper came on and, while slightly bored strutting her stuff, said to Barry, "You look fed up. What's up with you?" He replied, "You'd be fed up if you'd come two hundred miles to see your team lose a cup final in the last minute." Whilst continuing to reveal nearly all she carried on quizzing him as to what game it was and which team he supported.'

Bob Harrison's recollection is that, over the evening, our

group gradually split up, presumably as some chose to try and catch earlier trains home. He and I returned on the midnight special having had a final drink near Kings Cross. 'We went into a pub close by the station. It looked like a bomb had hit the place. We asked for a drink and the barman said, "No glasses left, lads. You'll have to find some." We managed to find some on a table and took them to the barman, who swiftly pulled two pints without washing them. Health and safety wasn't invented then. But, even more surprising, we didn't complain.' It seems, as had happened with our gang, a lot of people had chosen to go back on earlier trains than the midnight special. Harrison says, 'I remember getting on the train and being surprised at how few people were on it, considering it was packed to the rafters on the way down. We managed to find a compartment to ourselves and slept for most of the journey home.'

Neville Pierce from Normanton, a 13-year-old at the time, was among the Wakefield fans returning on one of the special trains. 'My mind goes back to Kings Cross station and boarding the 1.25 a.m. train back to Normanton. There was hardly a sound from the hundreds of fans on the platform and, once on the train, all talk were whispers, bodies never moved and young and old stared open-eyed into some far off distance. Not even the jolt of the train stopping at Peterborough, to throw the Sunday papers off, could break the Trinity supporters from their wide-eyed, pale-faced stares, thinking what might have been.'

Pierce recalls his feelings on getting back to the north. 'Arriving home about 5.30 a.m., the cold air of early morning had us all walking home ashen-faced, only to wake up later in the day to come to terms with what had happened that dramatic wet day at Wembley.' He also remembers the fans being praised for their good behaviour at the time. 'Later reports from British Rail regarding the five or six special trains that carried the Trinity fans was that not one single light bulb was missing and not one bit of damage was done to the trains. Football fans were vandalising trains around this time. The Trinity fans were too numb in body and soul to cause any damage.'

Trinity follower George Denton also has a particular memory of the way the fans of both Leeds and Wakefield conducted themselves on the return journey. 'What I found amazing was that we had a mixed train of Leeds and Wakefield supporters - half and half - and there wasn't one little bit of bother. They were all drinking beer together. They were all of the same opinion that the game should never, ever have been played, or at least put back some time to try to drain the ground.'

Roger Ingham and his mates were determined to have a good night out after the match despite the fact that their pal David Jeanes had ended up on the losing side. 'We always took the town by storm at night - someone had a bright idea that we'd go to a dog track at Chelsea. That was the 'early starter' and we'd have plenty of time for a night out in the West End. But again, typifying how it was raining, somebody said on the tube 'It might be off. Look at what it's been like here.' So we rang the ground up at Chelsea - it was on the old football field - and they said there were seagulls swimming on the pitch!'

Ingham and company had to make alternative arrangements and headed instead for the Saturday evening dog meeting at White City. 'Of course, they'd had the deluge there an' all. You've never seen a scene like it up there. The first two races - well, we left after that -it's the only time I've been to a dog meeting when you couldn't tell which were which. They were running round and splashing, like a dogs' swimming gala.'

Wakefield fan Gerry Wright was in the first year of a degree course at the University of Kent, in Canterbury. 'Coming from Stanley, near Wakefield, it was a bit of a culturally displacing experience.' Despite the imminence of his first year examinations he had attended the match with his father, two friends and their son. 'Unfortunately they were rabid Leeds fans and they had a son who was even more so than his parents. After the game, my father had to go back to Wakefield Westgate with his Leeds friends on the train. I travelled back to Canterbury. Both of us lacked close mutual support as a result. The son of my father's Leeds pals was not very magnanimous in victory and upset my father even more by saying to his own father, on arrival at Westgate, that they should, "leave the Trinity fans in their misery". My father never forgot that remark until the day he died and cheered every time Leeds suffered a defeat.'

Wright returned alone on the train to Canterbury that evening, like all Trinity supporters, disconsolate at what had happened at Wembley. 'The UKC [University of Kent, Canterbury] at that time was populated by minor public school students and Oxbridge rejects - very decent people but, of course, rugby league not on their radar. They were incapable of providing me with the emotional support I needed after such a traumatic afternoon. Despite the best efforts of Eddie Waring, rugby league was not on many people's agenda for Saturday afternoon watching there.'

Fortunately, Wright was supported by a university mate called Mike Maginnis who originated from Moseley, near Birmingham. Wright explains, 'He was aware of the game, saw most of it, could converse reasonably well on the subject and was sympathetic. He decided that the best support he could offer was a few pints, 'win or lose, get some booze' was his motto. He had a ticket for the Rutherford College disco and live gig. I think there was a big name on - it might even have been someone like Manfred Mann - but it could have been anybody for all I cared. All I wanted to do was talk about the game and get it out of my system. I just couldn't believe what I had seen and, of all clubs, to happen against Leeds. So, it was all a blur - and not just because of the alcohol - and all I wanted to do was just go through the game and become enveloped in a kind of catharsis, really.'

Wright attempted to chat to some women. As he puts it, 'they didn't seem to understand what I was saying - not only because of the alcohol and the northern accent - and were totally confused about why I was upset. Home counties accents proliferated and resonated with a, "How quaint: a northern game with such drama. What's the north like?" These were genuine comments. Some in those days had never been further north than Potters Bar. They may have been to Tanzania. They might have been to various parts of the world but some people thought the north was alien territory.'

Wright says that his friend Maginnis subsequently assured him that, 'the pulchritude on display was stunning and, at times according to Mike, certainly ought to have been something I was interested in.' But, after his experiences that day, Wright had other things on his mind. 'All I could talk about was Don Fox, the missed goal, the obstruction try, the rain, so I retired relatively early. And I'm not ashamed to admit it, I was emotionally broken. It was as though I'd experienced a bereavement. It might sound a bit sad, a bit shallow, but nonetheless it was the case. And it happened against Leeds. I keep coming back to this. It meant something in those days.'

For some who were present that day, getting back to the north wasn't without its problems. Doug Brammer, who had played professionally for Batley 'A' during his teens, was down at Wembley with his friends Dave Jenkinson and

They Walked on Water

Freddy Winterbottom. As an Ossett lad, from the borderlands between Wakefield and Dewsbury, he had always supported the Crown Flatt side so was not unduly troubled by the match result. With 'intro cards' for some West End clubs they wasted no time getting back into London and finished up in Oxford Circus around 12.30 a.m. Their taxi driver taking them back to their accommodation in Marylebone Square advised them that a 'beer festival', organised by a local rugby union club, was still underway near to the station and, perhaps unwisely, there they ended up.

Unsurprisingly, heads were less than clear the following morning. In the days before en-suite became the norm, Brammer went to another floor in the hotel for a bath and, on returning to their room, was confronted by Jenkinson and Winterbottom asking 'Have you any money?' Brammer knew that at the end of the previous night he had been left with just loose change but Jenkinson had lost his wallet, his driving licence and his watch and Winterbottom had also had his money taken by someone who had entered their room during the night.

Brammer recalls that, 'the main reception area was across the Square and there we headed to confront the proprietor - a Greek gentleman - whose first concern was whether we'd paid for our accommodation! A group of elderly women who were having breakfast nearby overheard our story. When I remarked that we could have been raped in our beds, one of them chipped in, "you'd have been better off; you'd have had some money left."' The police were called - to little effect - and, in an era long before 'holes in the wall,' the lads struggled to scrape together just enough for a sandwich each and the two gallons of petrol needed to top up the car tank to get them home.

Harry Jepson planned on staying in Huntingdon, breaking the journey back to the north. 'There were eight of us who went down and something went wrong with my car and I had to stay in Stamford all night. I had to call the RAC. and they took my car to a garage and said, "we can't do it today, Sunday, you'll have to stay overnight." I went with a lad called Michael Inman and he said, "I'll stay with you Harry," so I asked the garage man, "Anywhere we can stay?" "Yes," he said, "there's a nice pub." We went down to this pub and it fronted onto the boundary wall of Burleigh House which was 12 feet tall with those flat Peterborough bricks. We went down for a drink before we went to bed and there were a few old codgers in the pub and we began talking and I commented on the wall. And one old fella said, "Yes, my grandad worked on that wall." He said they'd started it when he was born and they hadn't finished it when he died. He said he worked on it all his life and he'd lived in a tied cottage owned by Lord Burleigh who became the Marquis of Exeter and was the 1924 Olympic gold medal winner in the hurdles. He told me his grandfather never went out of Stamford and he'd had the job all his life. Twice a year he went up to the big house for a meal and was given products of the house - vegetables, things like that. It wasn't quite the post-match conversation I expected to be having.'

Bearing in mind that, after doing a day's work and starting drinking in the Mitre pub in Wakefield at 7.30 p.m. on the Friday evening and having had no sleep before catching the 11.30 p.m. 'special' train back from Kings Cross the following evening, it is little surprise that the recollections of Eric Timmins and his three friends of the journey home vary somewhat. Timmins remembers them being so tired that they slept through Wakefield's Kirkgate station where they should have got off. He says, however that Barry Lodge insists that Pud, whose father worked on the railways, had said the train would go from Kirkgate to Westgate, the other

They Walked on Water

Wakefield station, where it was easier for them to disembark. Unfortunately it didn't and, halfway through a second night without going to bed, they found themselves heading towards Normanton.

Looking back nearly four and a half decades, Timmins is at a loss to understand why the four of them didn't get off the train at Normanton but ended up in Castleford. 'Anyway, we all started off walking from Cas to Normanton. There were no taxis around and no mobile phones in those days. We got as far as Normanton Town Hall and me and Barry had had enough walking by then. The other two lads carried on walking to Wakey. We found a phone box and rang Barry's dad, a bit pensively, because it was still only about 7.00 a.m. on Sunday morning by then. Thankfully, he agreed to come for us, picked me and Barry up outside Normanton Town Hall and then picked up our two mates as we passed the Horse and Groom on the bottom of Heath Common.'

The Leeds team returned home on their coach on Sunday morning with the wives and girlfriends travelling separately, catching the 9.40 a.m. train from Kings Cross.

The Wakefield players remained in London over the weekend. Geoff Oakes remarks that in his experience of finals with Trinity, on the day after the match the players and their wives and girlfriends usually went either to Petticoat Lane market or London Zoo. He recalls that one of the most vivid memories of their 1960 visit to Wembley was when a lion at the Zoo urinated all over Ken Rollin. The Trinity party had congregated round the large cage with some of the players growling at it and giving it some grief. 'That's when Rollin copped it. We're all just watching the lion and it sprayed all over him, full blast.' Quite remarkably, apparently this wasn't the first time he had been soaked by a lion. It had also happened at a zoo in Birkenhead when he was fifteen.

Petticoat Lane was the chosen destination in '68 and Ian Brooke and Harold Poynton have a particular memory of scrum-half Ray Owen's humour that day being directed at the unfortunate Don Fox. 'Nobody blamed him at all,' Poynton says, 'except Ray Owen who said, "Go and get me a 12 bore." He was only joking.' On one of the market stalls Owen had bought a toy cap gun and Brooke relates what happened. 'He put it at the side of Don's head and it didn't go off! He said, "Bloody hell. Missed again!" I remember it so vividly. We were all rolling about with laughing, you know, and that's how we all treated it. To us it wasn't as serious as people have tried to make out, just one of those things.'

Fox's missed goal may, indeed, have been, 'just one of those things' but by the day after the final his newly acquired celebrity status meant that the media were in hot pursuit. Graham Chalkley was with him in London that day and remembers what happened. 'We were in a wine bar and the press were all over and everybody wanted Don Fox. He was having a drink, going outside, getting interviewed and going back in. There were cameras inside and they just wouldn't leave him alone. It was like paparazzi.'

The national interest in what had happened at Wembley reached such a level that there are suggestions Fox was invited to appear on that evening's *Sunday Night at the London Palladium*, which was broadcast nationwide on television. According to Chalkley, Fox said, 'No chance. I'm going back to the fans.' Ian Brooke believes that it was Shirley Bassey who was topping the bill that night. 'I think it did get a mention by Bruce Forsyth.' Fox's brother Neil says, 'All I know was they'd invited him to the London Palladium and I think they then re-ran it on the Monday. I think it was live on the Sunday and it came on our televisions on the Monday. When I saw it on the Monday, the compere mentioned Don in his little speech at the front.' The joke made at Fox's expense was more or less the same as Ray Owen's jest earlier in the day at Petticoat Lane. Neil Fox says the story was that his brother had gone into the dressing room after the match, got a gun and tried to shoot himself, 'But he missed again!'

According to Don Fox's son Greg, what actually happened is even more indicative of the impact on the nation. Apparently, on the Saturday evening after the game, a courier came from Buckingham Palace to Baileys Hotel with a message asking Fox to join the Queen, who had obviously seen coverage of the match on television, the following evening at the London Palladium. But, as he looked forward to returning home to his wife and young son, his priority was to stay with his team-mates and the fans rather than having an evening with the Monarch. Greg Fox makes the point, 'That's the sort of person my dad was. A lot of people would have jumped at the chance to go and see the Queen.'

On the Sunday evening, rather than being at the Palladium, Fox went out for drinks in London with his team-mates. His brother, Neil, says that the Trinity players asked Don where he wanted to go. He chose the Prospect of Whitby pub which he had previously visited with some lads he used to go out with. 'And we said, "If Don wants that, we'll all go." We got about four or five taxis. And I think the pub was closed because it was Sunday! We all had to come back to the Piccadilly area.'

Away from the dramas of Wembley that weekend - the celebrations and commiserations - other events were occurring back in Wakefield. One person with more reason than most to remember the date is Michael Newsome. It was the day he was born, and, as his father, John, puts it, 'That's something else Don Fox gets blamed for!' A Trinity supporter from being a young boy, John Newsome gained considerable distinction as an international long distance runner, representing Great Britain four times, winning the race on each occasion. He won twenty-eight open road races and took part in a total of thirty-two marathons, winning ten of them and has been a prominent parish and district councillor in the Wakefield area over many years. His wife, Wendy, has also followed Trinity from a young age, with the couple's engagement ring being bought from Holmes Jewellers in Westgate, Wakefield, on the way to a match at Belle Vue.

Michael was John and Wendy Newsome's second son and had been due to be born on the weekend prior to the Wembley final. The couple watched the match at Wendy's parents' house in George-a-Green Road, Lupset, where she was well aware that the baby's appearance was imminent. 'I was having twinges,' she recalls. 'I knew something was going to happen because I was having them all through the match. I actually sat watching the game going, "don't come yet, please don't come yet."' John remembers being, 'far too engrossed in the match to worry about what was going on.' Wendy says, 'I got through it and Michael was born at six o'clock in the evening, just after the match had finished.'

At a time when fathers were not encouraged to be present at births, John, a primary school teacher, was downstairs at his in-laws doing some marking after the match had ended. There were also no foetal scans during pregnancies so there was more of a surprise element in giving birth then than is often the case nowadays. Wendy remembers, 'When Michael was born he just gave a little yelp and the midwife wasn't happy so she slapped him. He gave another yelp and downstairs my dad turned round and said, "it's twins."' As John recollects, 'That did worry me!' Although Michael Newsome has obviously no recollection of the match that day, one of his proudest possessions is a programme from the 1968 Rugby League Challenge Cup final on the day he was born.

While the Newsomes - unable to get to Wembley - at least had the consolation of watching the match on television, another lifelong Trinity supporter, Mike Rylance, knew nothing of the result and drama of the final until several days after it had happened. Son of Trinity legend Ron Rylance and author of *The Forbidden Game*, the story of the banning of rugby league by the French Vichy government, he was on holiday in St. Tropez when the match took place. 'There was no television coverage over there and I knew absolutely nothing about what had happened until I found an English newspaper a week later.'

Chapter Seventeen

And losers shout loudest

The victorious Leeds team were given a civic reception following their return home on the day after the final, arriving at Leeds Civic Hall in an open-top coach, where thousands were waiting to welcome them. The *Daily Express* reported that, 'A thousand people lined the route from the coach station to the city centre. There were two thousand outside the Civic Hall and more cheering fans on the balcony of Leeds Infirmary.' The Rugby League Challenge Cup was, according to the press, '...given a place of honour in the Banqueting Hall.' Having been the first to commiserate with Don Fox after his goal miss at the end of the match, speaking at the reception, Leeds skipper, Mick Clark, made clear how sorry he felt for Fox over what had happened. 'I wouldn't have wished a miss like that on my worst enemy,' he was reported as saying.

Albert Eyre has a clear memory of how he felt on the team's return to Leeds. 'When we got back on the Sunday night I was absolutely exhausted with everything.' But for him and most of the other players involved there would be no lie-in the following morning. They were all part-time professionals in the days before Super League and had a living to earn, in Eyre's case, as a flag-layer. 'I went to work on the Monday because I was self-employed. I had to go.'

There was also a massive turn out of Wakefield folk as Trinity returned from London on the Monday following the final. Neil Fox says the welcome the team received, 'was just like we'd won the Cup. We got off the train at Westgate and they brought us out up Westgate and up Wood Street. You couldn't believe the number of people out there. There must have been 30,000 lining from the station right the way up to the Town Hall.'

Harold Poynton remembers that day as perhaps putting the Wembley defeat into perspective. 'It was a marvellous day, really. I mean, you can't live forever thinking about the match. There was a good crowd to greet us.' Even as, like Poynton, also a veteran of the 1963 Wembley victory over Wigan, Ian Brooke was moved by the response of the fans. 'The amount of Wakefield people out on the streets was astonishing, you didn't realise the fan base until you actually made that journey from Westgate station to the Town Hall in Beverley's Brewery wagon. Everybody was out cheering and it was as good as '63. To say we'd lost, it didn't seem like it because of the welcome.'

Harold Poynton's wife Cath says the Trinity players' wives and girlfriends returned from London separately and were reunited with them at the Town Hall reception. 'I remember coming up Wood Street, we had to walk up the road because they were just packed.' The banners that greeted Trinity's short journey on a red, white and blue decorated brewery lorry that evening clearly evidenced a shared anger amongst the team's supporters over the manner of the defeat. 'We were robbed by the ref' said one, while another read 'Hebblethwaite for Vietnam.' Neil Fox remembers the crowd wanting to see the Trinity players after they had entered the Town Hall. 'The one they particularly wanted to see and have a few words with was Don. They were shouting for him because he was intimating that he was going to retire. When he heard the crowd shouting his name outside the Town Hall, I think that changed his mind.'

I have a particular memory of the crowd chanting for Don Fox and giving him the most wonderful welcome when he came out onto the balcony with his wife, Mary. Inside the Town Hall, according to Geoff Oakes, there was more than a little gallows humour. 'They were all shouting, "We want Don. We want Don." We went, aye, they're gonna bleeding hang him!' But they didn't, and the response he got from the Wakefield fans that evening did indeed persuade him to continue playing the next season.

Mick Morgan remembers that for him and Trinity hooker George Shepherd the dramas of that memorable weekend didn't end with the Town Hall reception. 'I left the function and went with George and his missus in the car. He was taking me home but we called for a beer at Wragby somewhere. We ended up pulling left hand into the car park and a car hit us from behind. It was a school teacher who'd been invited to the do. He'd had a beer or two and George just took the details and let it ride. I thought that's put the kybosh on it. That's finished the weekend off!'

For Don Fox, that weekend's events continued to be relived through the intense media interest. Perhaps the most memorable televised image of him subsequently were the shots taken at Featherstone Rovers' Post Office Road ground, where he was filmed kicking goals in his carpet slippers. His family also featured in some of the publicity. Greg Fox says his mother still has an image of him taken by a newspaper photographer at the time. 'I think the press put some sticks up in the garden and got me kicking a rugby ball over them. It got published in the paper. Actually, looking back, it's probably not a wise thing to have done. I can't remember what my dad said about it.'

The repercussions of this match were the subject of vigorous local debate, leading to rumour and counter-rumour in the Wakefield area relating to the perceived partiality of referee Hebblethwaite. I certainly recall hearing from a number of different sources that John Hebblethwaite was related to one of the Leeds players in their Wembley side that day. Other Wakefield supporters vented their anger at the way the Leeds based media had failed to reflect how desperately unlucky Trinity had been. Somewhere, I still have in my possession a spoof report from the Leeds-based *Yorkshire Evening Post*, presumably penned by a Trinity supporter, purporting to give an account of the Challenge Cup final in which Wakefield had defeated Leeds 117-0. The report's headline was, 'unlucky Leeds.'

Another Wakefield resident, the part-time TV actress Frances Cox, who appeared in various programmes including *Coronation Street*, *Last of the Summer Wine* and *Open All Hours*, was even moved to poetry over the affair. Her lengthy piece, published in the *Wakefield Express*, included reference to the controversial obstruction try:

> *So why did the referee call,*
> *Advantage to Wakefield's opponents?*
> *When all the chap did was to fall.*
> *Extending his arms as he did so,*
> *Momentum impelling him on,*
> *To save himself sliding to nowhere,*

Perhaps he'd skid close to someone?
A penalty would have been wiser,
If Hebblethwaite only had tried,
To form a considered decision,
And pocket his referee's pride.

The public consciousness - of Wakefield folk at least - had been raised by not only what they had witnessed during the match but, in particular, by subsequent media reports of the refereeing controversy surrounding the obstruction try. 'Arguments rage after Leeds win,' was the *Yorkshire Evening Post* headline on the Monday after the match in a report which focussed on the controversy around the obstruction try. 'This, not the Fox miss, is the real talking point,' it claimed. The anger of Trinity officials about this issue had received considerable coverage in the aftermath of the match. 'Row mars Leeds joy,' was the headline of a *Daily Sketch* story the same day. It reported that, 'Wakefield will never believe that the try should have been given by referee Hebblethwaite and they are considering protesting to the Rugby League.' The *Sun* also claimed, 'Wakefield may report referee John Hebblethwaite to the Rugby League.'

'Trinity protest over unholy try,' was the headline of a *Daily Mail* piece at the start of the week after the final. It noted, 'Wakefield Trinity are to make an official protest over the controversial refereeing decision behind Leeds' record eighth success in the Challenge Cup final.' The paper's rugby league correspondent Brian Batty recorded that Trinity chairman John Ridge had stated the previous evening, 'We just can't take an issue like this lying down for too much is at stake. We shall hold a meeting on Tuesday and put our protest to the League.' Batty added that Ridge had also alleged that an earlier offence had been missed by the referee

in the run-up to the incident. 'Atkinson knocked on as he
went for the ball and as far as obstruction goes it was
impossible to say whether he would have scored in such
appalling conditions.'

On the team's return to Wakefield that Monday
evening, Ridge continued to raise his concerns over what had
happened during the final. 'We lost the cup because of that
diabolical decision of the referee,' he was reported as saying
to the *Wakefield Express*, 'but there is nothing we can do about
it except to register our strongest protest.' Coach Ken Traill
added, 'We weren't robbed so much as absolutely done out
of it. However that's football. Only one side can win and we
have to take it.' Ian Brooke recalls that at the Town Hall
reception referee Hebblethwaite's name was mentioned in
perhaps every speech. 'Nowadays, you wouldn't be able to
say it, but in those days nobody said anything.'

Well, it seems they did. These remarks - probably made
in the heat of the moment in the aftermath of a bitter and
controversial defeat, but reported in the press - were to result
in a lengthy wrangle between Wakefield and the governing
body which never seems to have become public knowledge.
None of the players involved in the 1968 final to whom I have
spoken were aware of what subsequently happened in the
Chapeltown Road, Leeds boardroom where the sport was
administered, over the following four months.

While I have found no record of Wakefield Trinity
making formal representations regarding their concerns over
the refereeing, the minutes of the meeting of the Rugby
League Council, held on Wednesday, 26th June, 1968, refer to
two items relating to the 1968 final. Item four noted an
agreement to allow the Leeds club to purchase an extra cup
winner's medal for coach, Roy Francis, and Trinity to
purchase extra runners-up medals for five players; Neil Fox,

Joe Bonnar, Geoff Oakes, David Garthwaite and Gerry Round - who had played in earlier cup rounds. Trinity were also given permission to buy runners-up medals for Chairman John Ridge, Secretary Eddie Thomas and Coach, Ken Traill.

Under the heading 'Challenge Cup final', the next paragraph - item five - read as follows:-

> *A letter from Mr. J.P. Hebblethwaite was read regarding remarks published in the press and alleged to have been made by Mr. J. Ridge (Chairman of Wakefield Trinity) and Mr. K. Traill (Coach of Wakefield Trinity) relating to the control of the Wembley cup final by Mr. J.P. Hebblethwaite. It was agreed that this matter be referred to the Management Committee.*

Other than noting the receipt of a letter of thanks from the Private Secretary of the Duke of Kent - chief guest at the game - there are no other references in the minutes to the remarkable events of 11 May, 1968.

It may have had no bearing whatsoever on John Hebblethwaite's decision to pursue his grievance against Ridge and Traill but, only a fortnight before what surely should have been the highlight of his refereeing career, he had found himself being strongly attacked in the press over his conduct as a touch judge during a match played on 25th April between local York amateur teams, the Derwent Arms and Irish National League, in the semi-final of the York Rugby League Interworks Cup. The match, according to a *York Evening Press* report, 'had been marred by violence on the field, and police were called when a threatening crowd of more than 60 spectators gathered.' It went on, 'Rugby League Cup final referee, Mr. John Hebblethwaite, who was acting as a touch judge, was involved in an incident with a spectator.'

They Walked on Water

The match had been refereed by Gerry Kershaw, who went on to become a Grade One referee, involved in many top level matches. There were dismissals and a significant number of injuries as a consequence of on-field incidents but particular controversy arose at full-time, with the score at eleven-all. According to the press, 'the referee…ordered extra time to be played. Derwent refused because, they claimed, the rules stated there should be a replay. The team was then disqualified. It is understood that an ugly crowd then milled about, and that Mr. Hebblethwaite was involved in an incident.'

A letter published in part in the *York Evening Press* two days later implied that Hebblethwaite had been largely responsible for the crowd trouble at this match. Written by a C. Melia of Osbaldwick it stated, 'To see a player lying injured, unattended on the field after a particularly nasty incident was nauseating enough, but for him to lie there for a full five minutes while a petty wrangle developed over a remark which could not have raised objections at a children's tea party, "You'll have to do better than that at Wembley, John," is pathetic.'

It is, perhaps, important to put this incident in the context of rugby league during the 1960s. I certainly have a clear memory of police intervening during an on-field brawl in a Trinity match at Belle Vue during that period, but the professional game, while much more unruly than nowadays, was usually somewhat more disciplined than at amateur level. I had moved from playing intermediate to open-age amateur rugby league in the late sixties when mass brawls and abandonments were by no means unusual. Indeed, if the early scrums of a match at that time had passed without a vigorous exchange of fists, it would have been deemed remarkable. The amateur competition in which Kershaw and

Hebblethwaite sought to officiate at the time would undoubtedly have tested their patience.

Even though John Hebblethwaite was a first grade referee, it is unlikely that the Rugby Football League's Management Committee were made aware of what was alleged to have happened during this match when their next meeting was held during the afternoon of Tuesday 23rd July at headquarters. The specific circumstances of the post Wembley public criticism referee Hebblethwaite received was given particular attention. The first item of 'other business' that day concerned the matter referred to the Committee by the Council and was headed, 'Wakefield Trinity - Criticisms of Cup final Referee'. It is perhaps worth noting that the lack of the word 'alleged' in respect of what was, at this point, an unproven complaint may offer some indication of the official view of the strength of Hebblethwaite's case against Trinity.

The Management Committee minutes record in detail the proceedings concerning the matter.

A letter from Referee, Mr. J.P. Hebblethwaite, was re-read. In this letter, Mr. Hebblethwaite complained about adverse criticisms of his refereeing of the Cup final which had been published in the Press and which had been attributed to Mr. J. Ridge, Chairman of Wakefield Trinity, and Mr. K. Traill, Coach. A letter from Mr. J. Ridge was read. Mr. K. Traill was admitted to the meeting.

The Chairman asked Mr. Traill if he had any doubts as to the powers of the Management Committee to deal with the matter and in reply Mr. Traill acknowledged the authority of the Committee.

He admitted referring to a decision made by the Cup final Referee as 'diabolical', a statement which had been subsequently published in the Press. Mr. Traill contended that he had said this in the dressing-rooms and it was not said directly to the Press.

Mr. Traill retired and was recalled to be informed of the decisions of the Committee which were as follows:-

The Committee noted that Mr. K. Traill's explanation was that the alleged criticism of the referee was in the privacy of the dressing-rooms but the Committee felt that if Wakefield Trinity allowed members of the Press into the dressing-rooms then the club officials were responsible for any remarks made to the Press in those rooms. The Committee decided to reprimand Mr. K. Traill and demand from him an assurance in writing that he would not repeat the offence.

While Neil Fox has no recollection of any dressing room remarks by Traill or Ridge he certainly believes it was likely there would have been press in with the players after the match. 'There would have been reporters, because they'd go in both dressing rooms asking things. It was quite normal.' David Jeanes also confirms that it was not in any way unusual for press reporters to be in the Trinity dressing rooms in his experience: 'Press always used to come in - Brian Batty and Jack Bentley and whoever else.' His recollection of what happened after this final was that the media interest was very much in the losing team's camp rather than that of the victors. 'They obviously spent more time, I think, with us than what they did with Leeds. Don was the story when really the penalty try was the story.'

The exact contents of the letter sent by Trinity Chairman John Ridge to the Management Committee about the events after the final are not disclosed in the minutes for that day but his arguments, whatever they were, do not appear to have convinced the members.

> *Mr. J. Ridge did not appear before the Committee. In his case the Committee felt most strongly that his explanation was most unsatisfactory and it was decided that Mr. J. Ridge be severely reprimanded and warned as to his future conduct. He was also instructed to submit an assurance in writing that he would not repeat the offence.*

It is perhaps worth noting that the next minute involved Wakefield Trinity being fined £50 for having signed Stuart Carlton of Normanton while still a schoolboy. The RFL archives of this period also indicate that Trinity were involved in a lengthy wrangle with the Council and Management Committee over an alleged breach of bye-laws concerning the circumstances of the registration of a player named Bainbridge. This matter was not resolved until, over a year later, Trinity finally pleaded guilty to three offences of contravening bye-laws.

Whether these other ongoing matters had any bearing on the Management Committee's approach to the allegations against Ridge and Traill is open to debate but it is clear that what they were deemed to have done after the final had also ruffled other feathers. Item 13 of the Management Committee minutes for the same meeting was headed, 'Senior Referees Association' and included the following paragraph:-

> *It was noted that the Senior Referees Association deplored the public criticisms attributed to Wakefield Trinity officials regarding the Cup final Referee.*

They Walked on Water

The Management Committee's next meeting was held during the afternoon of Thursday 12th September, in the Piccadilly Hotel, Manchester, and the minutes record that the first item under 'matters arising' concerned the aftermath of the Cup final.

> *Letters from Messrs Ridge and Traill, Chairman and Coach of Wakefield Trinity, were read giving an assurance to the Committee that they would not repeat the offence of making public adverse criticisms of referees of matches in which their club had taken part. Receipt of the letters was noted.*

Officially, at least, this appears to have been the end of the matter but it wasn't the last occasion at which the Management Committee dealt with an issue concerning the refereeing of John Hebblethwaite. At their meeting at RFL headquarters on the afternoon of Tuesday 4th March, 1969, under an item concerning 'referees reports', the Secretary referred to a lengthy missive from the St. Helens club regarding Hebblethwaite.

> *The report stated that the appointment (to referee their match) had evidently been made without 'consideration'. The Secretary pointed out that the official in question had been appointed by the Council to referee the last Cup final and that apparently the marks given by clubs on that official were very much above average…*

Every referee will face their fair share of controversies and John Hebblethwaite certainly had his in 1968. For him, few can have faced the enormity of the decision he took to give the go-ahead for the final in the most appalling weather. Nor faced the genuine prospect of having to decide on an abandonment as the weather deteriorated around half time and during the second half. And, as if that wasn't enough, few can have been publicly accused - as he clearly was by David Coleman - of having gifted a match to the winning side.

Chapter Eighteen

The tragic post-script

For the Rugby Football League, the 1968 Challenge Cup final would have been regarded as a highly successful occasion. Its controversies gained the sport considerable media coverage and the attendance of 87,100 was excellent at a time when they had serious concerns over declining crowds and the impact of the live televising of matches.

The Annual Report submitted to the Rugby League Council's 1968 AGM noted that gate receipts had totalled £56,171.16s.6d. Other income from the match included the BBC sound fee of £105.0.0, the BBC TV fee of £4,000.0.0, and the BBC facilities fee of £10.10s.0d. There was additional income of £62.10s.0d.arising from the value of space for TV cameras and an ITN facilities fee of £5.5s.0d. From the total income of over £60,000 from the event, the winners, runners-up and losing semi-finalists were to share £27,771.19s.3d.

For Wakefield Trinity, what they received from the match scarcely compensated them for the highly controversial defeat which was to be a watershed in the club's history. The word 'tragic' has been used on many occasions to describe Don Fox's last minute goal miss but, sadly, it is difficult to avoid the fact that genuine tragedy did follow the 1968 Challenge Cup decider. There is little doubt that the Wakefield team and their supporters held John Hebblethwaite - and not Fox - entirely responsible for Trinity's failure to land the double in 1968. The memory of what happened would not easily be eradicated. Indeed, many years later the controversies around his performance in the middle were institutionalised in the *Yorkshire Post* when their columnist, the author Roger Cross, a Wakefield man it has to be said, initiated the Hebblethwaite Myopia Award for highly questionable refereeing decisions.

But surely no-one would have wished upon John Hebblethwaite the tragic events which were to befall his family within a matter of weeks of the Wembley final. On 28th July, at their family home in Ostman Road, Acomb, York, his 47-year-old wife Winifred was found dead following an overdose of Butobarbitone and Methaqualone. John Hebblethwaite told a subsequent inquest, held in York on 19th August that Mrs. Hebblethwaite had experienced abdominal and head pains over many years and these had gradually worsened.

The inquest was told that very heavy amounts of sleeping tablets were found in her body by a pathologist and the Coroner, Mr. Innes Ware, expressed the view that Mrs. Hebblethwaite must have obtained such an amount by accumulating them instead of throwing them away. Recording a verdict of suicide, Mr. Ware issued a warning that people should destroy old tablets, rather than leaving them around the house, '...especially where people are unwell.'

Some eight months after his wife's death and less than

a year after the controversies of the 1968 final, referee Hebblethwaite himself was dead. At the RFL AGM held 28th May, 1969, the minutes noted on page 5:-

> *The Council reports with deep regret the deaths during the season of Mr. J. A. Phillips, the former Bradford Northern player, Chairman and Council Member and Mr. J. P. Hebblethwaite, the referee of last year's Cup final.*

Around the time of John Hebblethwaite's death, on 16th April 1969, in a caravan at Primrose Valley, near Filey, Ridge and Traill had been reprimanded for their attacks on his handling of the 1968 final and, only a few weeks before, he had been the subject of a critical report from St. Helens. It is impossible to determine whether such attacks on his performance, during a period that would have probably been the peak of his refereeing career, had any bearing on his decision to take his own life. His representations to the Rugby League Council indicate that he was obviously sensitive to comment.

Like, but on a much lesser scale to football, the referee and his role was perhaps no longer being seen as sacrosanct and respect eroded. Former Wakefield mayor, Norman Hazell, for example, recalls a conversation with the Leeds first grade referee, George Philpott, with whom he worked at Yorkshire Copperworks in the city.

'I attended the 1967 Championship final at Headingley when Wakefield Trinity were playing St. Helens and George awarded an obstruction try which meant the game finished as a draw. We talked about it afterwards and he told me on the Monday how concerned he was because of the nasty threats that had been sent to his home. His wife was really frightened. Referees are like cricket umpires and get used to quite a bit of abuse, but George, in fairness to his wife, asked the Rugby League if he could withdraw from the replay. Traditionally, if there's a draw, the replay's taken by the same referee but, in this case, poor George was replaced.'

The BBC commentator, columnist and author Ray French captained the Saints side that day in a match which - like the 1968 final - was played on a soaking pitch in thunderstorms. Writing about the game many years later, he recalled that not only was the obstruction try - awarded to Trinity's Ray Owen - highly controversial, but, earlier in the contest, the referee had, '…disallowed what appeared to be a perfectly good try to our winger Tony Barrow.' French confirms Hazell's recollection that referee Philpott's decisions, '… sadly prompted such threatening letters to him and his family that he stood down in the replay in favour of experienced whistler Joe Manley.'

There is no evidence that Hebblethwaite or his family were subject to similar threats at this time although it is by no means inconceivable given the anger aimed in his direction by the Trinity club and clearly apparent among the team's fans at the homecoming. On top of the quite recent loss of his wife there were, however, clearly other matters troubling him at the time.

The *York Evening Press* of 17th April 1969 reported that following his death, a charge against him of stealing a tinned steak and kidney pie worth 3s. 6d had been withdrawn that day by York police. Solicitor, Mr. Peter Gildener, who was due to represent Hebblethwaite was noted as stating that, 'In view of certain recent publicity in the press and television, I feel it is necessary to point out that I had full instructions to deny the charge that was being made today.'

At the opening of the inquest into John Hebblethwaite's death, at Filey the same day, it was reported that he had been found dead in his caravan after the police had been handed some letters he had sent. A press account stated that, 'P.C. David Robinson said he found Mr. Hebblethwaite lying on a bed with ...beer and capsules nearby. A small tin containing white substance was found in the fire grate.'

The inquest was adjourned until 29th April when the Deputy Coroner for the Buckrose District, Mr. Dennis Howard, recorded a verdict that Hebblethwaite had killed himself. The court heard that he had written at least nine letters, posted on the day he died, to his solicitor, doctor and various friends, before poisoning himself with a cyanide meat sandwich. A pathologist had determined that an amount of cyanide, many times the fatal dose, had been swallowed and the inquest learned that it was likely that Hebblethwaite had obtained it from his previous employment as an instrument maker at the 41 Command REME workshops at Strensall.

John Hebblethwaite's elder son, Peter, had the painful task of giving evidence at the inquest, indicating that his father had been very depressed since the death of his wife the previous year. He identified statements written by his father which confirmed that the loss of Winifred was a key factor in him determining to take his own life and evidence was given that he had been treated for depression. Whether the pending court case had any bearing is unclear but, in a statement at the inquest, Mr. Howard said, 'I want to make it clear that the letters written by Mr. Hebblethwaite do not refer to those proceedings.'

Looking back on these sad events over forty years later, David Hebblethwaite, the referee's younger son, does not believe that the controversies around the 1968 final played any part in his death. But he does feel that the fact he was having to retire from top class refereeing, because of his age, at the time was very significant.

'My dad was heartbroken,' David says about his father's reaction to the loss of his wife. 'I think he knew it was the end, or coming up to the end. He'd lost my mam and he was going to lose his rugby league as well.'

Chapter Nineteen

Living with the legacy

The author of the centenary history of Wakefield Trinity, John Lindley, was strongly of the view that Don Fox should not be held responsible for the 1968 defeat. 'Whilst it is true that goalkickers can win matches, they surely cannot lose them. Defeat is already shown on the scoreboard when the goalkicker takes the stage - and whilst he has the power to change such a verdict into a draw or a victory, should he miss that chance his failure does not cause him to bring about the defeat, only to confirm it.'

Unfortunately, not many people have seen fit to reflect on what happened at the end of that match quite as charitably and Fox's miss, with its consequences, has achieved legendary status for its ignominy.

It says something about the notoriety of what happened at the end of that match in 1968 that, more than fifteen years later on 20th October, 1983, when Neil Fox was at Buckingham Palace receiving his MBE, the last second goal miss would get a mention as he met the Queen. 'There's not a lot of conversation,' he says. 'We had to go in front of her and just bow. And she said, "You're the rugby player." I said, "Yes, Ma'am." And she said, "But you're not the one who…?" I said, "No Ma'am. That was my brother." I think she was going to say "…who missed the goal?" Because, obviously, she must have known and read about it. And then she said "Congratulations," shook my hand. That's what she does and I've seen it since on television. She shakes your hand and just pushes your hand back as though that's your time. You are told this before you go up. But she knew about Don.'

Don Fox's playing career at Trinity ended in the spring of 1970 when he transferred to Batley for a nominal fee. He subsequently coached the Batley 'A' team and, in late 1972, was appointed the club's senior coach. According to his biographer Ron Bailey, 'He was not entirely comfortable in a coaching role,' resigning in late 1974. Neil, says, 'He wasn't cut out to be a coach, wasn't Don. I think he was too quiet.' Peter Fox agrees. 'Our Don wasn't a talker about the game. He wasn't a talker about tactics, because he used to do everything off the cuff. He'd a brilliant mind. He used to do things on the field that no other player would think about. That was our Don's style of play.'

But, despite being widely admired by many as arguably the finest player of his generation, for the rest of his life he would be unable to escape the fact that a brilliant sporting career was so often remembered for just one brief moment of failure. His son Greg says, 'The thing that my dad was not happy about on the day is that he got the man of the match and, obviously, it was overshadowed by what happened at the end, the final kick. It was just one small part of his career - a very distinguished career - and they don't remember that. The people who don't know about rugby always refer to this match. The people who know about rugby - genuinely know about rugby - knew my dad for being a great player, so he's not remembered for just that kick. But, obviously, the kick was quite a poignant moment in rugby league, especially with Eddie Waring's commentary and everything. It's something he certainly lived with.'

Greg Fox obviously has no memory of seeing his father play but is clearly angered that his place in history is confined by many to one particular inglorious incident. 'People don't remember what a playmaker he was. They just remember him for this kick and that's the unfortunate thing.' Mick Morgan witnessed his long career at close hand and strongly reiterates these concerns over a marvellous sporting career being narrowed down to the 1968 incident. 'I was Featherstone born and bred and Don Fox was my hero. I've stood behind the sticks at Post Office Road and watched him. But sadly, whenever the BBC are showing anything historical about rugby league, the missed conversion always comes on. But Don Fox was the best footballer I've ever seen in my life.'

As someone who saw the latter stages of Fox's playing career at Featherstone Rovers and all his time at Wakefield Trinity, I would entirely concur with Morgan's assessment. I can think of no-one in that era who had his ability to control and change a game and it is surely no coincidence that the only time in Trinity's very distinguished history that they won the Championship - in 1967 and 1968 - was during Don Fox's time at the club. His brother, Neil, who clearly played a role in persuading Wakefield to sign him, recalls, 'The Committee said: "What do you want your Don for?" I said "Because he's the best player in the game today."'

Every top-level participant in sport will have their share of ups and downs. Indeed life as a whole for most of us will contain its share of positives and negatives. But those downs, negatives and failures do not usually recur time and time again, in the public eye, for all to see. For Fox, it was different. The many successes became distant history but the '68 miss was ever present. The grainy, black and white footage of the goal miss and Fox prostrate on the ground in despair has been run over and over again, to the extent that it is almost a fixture during the BBC's Challenge Cup coverage. When, in 1975, BBC television was celebrating twenty years of its Saturday sports show, *Grandstand*, included as their rugby league memory from an archive of hundreds of matches over the two decades were the last few moments of 1968.

That goal miss has even been used in a television advertisement, commercially capitalising on one individual's awful moment of failure. I remember talking to Don about it and offering, while I was in the Commons, to make formal representations. I felt there was a strong case for the Advertising Standards Authority to look at the issue and the use being made of an intense personal tragedy to basically make money. But Fox was resigned to it by then. He knew full well that if this particular piece was taken off air it would only crop up again somewhere else.

As well as constant televised reminders of the moment, Fox also had to get used to being featured in numerous press pieces on '68. One in the *Independent on Sunday*, on 25th April 1999 actually started, 'Alright, let's remind him about it again.' *The Sun* included it in a feature entitled, 'The greatest sporting blunders of all time,' and in October 2002, the *Sunday Times* had it in the top ten of the biggest mistakes in international sport. It was listed as number nineteen in the *Observer*'s January 2007 list of fifty 'Heartbreaking Moments' and, as the old Empire stadium was making way for the new Wembley, the incident was listed among the 'Triumphs and disasters [which] moulded [the] character of a regal London institution' in the *Daily Telegraph* on 28th March 2005. Don found himself classed in the anxiety stakes, alongside Fanny Blankers-Koen, a Dutch athlete in the 1948 London Olympic Games who won the hurdles in a very close finish with Britain's Maureen Gardner. 'I thought she had won when they started playing the [British] National Anthem. But it was for the arrival of the Queen.'

More than forty-four years on from the 1968 final, Fox's miss was featured in the *Mail Online* in an article on, 'Sporting misses that changed history for all the wrong reasons.' Mark Lawford's article suggested, 'Rugby League is not everyone's cup of tea but the 1968 Rugby League Challenge Cup final between Wakefield and Leeds was one of those moments that made *Grandstand* great.'

So 11th May 1968, was never allowed to fade into the distance for Don Fox and many of those who knew him well saw this as a factor in his lengthy battle with depression in later life. His former Featherstone Rovers colleague and good friend Joe Mullaney recalled to the *Yorkshire Post*, 'That missed goal changed Don. He didn't seem to dwell on it but the press were always referring to it and I have no doubt it contributed to his illness in later life.'

According to his fellow prop David Jeanes, '...it seemed as if it got a bigger and bigger burden on Don's mind. Obviously, the press never helped it. It's still now classed in anything to do with sport as the number one miss. How do you live with that? He never got over it and it was awful to see how he went down. You'd go somewhere and you'd meet him. You could never discuss it. You would try and talk to him. It wasn't that his life finished then - it didn't finish - but he went on a downward spiral. It was a big, big factor.'

Ian Brooke is certainly aware of the effect on Fox's subsequent life. 'I think for the few years afterwards, while he was still playing, it never really got to him. It was only in later life, when he reflected on it.' As Brooke remarks, there were always these regular reminders of his goal kicking failure. 'The problem was that people brought things out - there was a DVD about 100 tries and one missed goal. And it was all a money-making ruse about Don's failure and to be able to live with that, it takes a strong person to do that. I'm not saying Don wasn't strong - he was - but I wouldn't like anyone to go through that all those times.'

Perhaps of most concern, to those in the Trinity camp at least, is the highly selective nature of the oft-repeated clip with, usually, just the Hirst try and, sometimes, just the Fox miss implying that this was the historical totality of this remarkable final. Brooke reflects on his comments to Fox after yet another showing. 'I used to say to him, "Don, the obstruction try ought to be alongside that as a miscarriage of justice." But they never do and everybody forgets it.'

Brooke speaks with very real passion about what he sees as the effect on Fox over very many years of a genuine injustice. 'That's my burning thing in life. The significant moment was the obstruction try because it wouldn't have mattered about that kick because the try would never have been. But that's how history is and how things are formed and how it goes on in legend forever.'

The BBC regularly repeated that clip in a way that also apparently disturbed Eddie Waring. His nephew Harry remembers a conversation he had with him some twelve years after.

'Eddie and I were discussing some of the matches he'd witnessed and the subject came round to the 'Watersplash final' and the Don Fox missed goal. Eddie said that he always regretted saying those words 'the poor lad'. They were the first thing that came into his head - that he painted the picture as he saw it - but, because of Don's mental problems, Eddie always felt that he may have had some influence over his deterioration. I don't think that's the case, but Eddie felt that.'

Harold Poynton's rugby league career spanned a similar period to Don Fox's and he had known him over many years. 'I played against him at school. I played for Wakefield City Schools. He played for Pontefract and Cas. He was never the same, I didn't think so. He was never the same again.' And, perhaps more than most, the Leeds winger John Atkinson felt very deeply for what Fox had to face up to over subsequent years. 'You see I sympathised later on in life because I've suffered from clinical depression since I was a kid. I had to come out of the police with it. I didn't know, in those days, what it was all about. But I know the massive effect it had on him. As far as Don was concerned, he'd not only let his team down, he let the whole of Wakefield down.'

But Peter Fox and those who were particularly close to Don are clearly of the view that his depression in later life was unrelated to the events of 1968. Peter says, 'Our Don was always a lad that kept himself to himself. He never spoke to anybody about anything, to my knowledge, that made him depressed. We didn't know what was making him upset but he always took things to heart did our Don. He was always a serious lad. He wasn't a jester, a joker.'

Coming originally from Streethouse, near Sharlston, the village between Wakefield and Featherstone which Fox hailed from and having gone to the same school, Ken Rollin knew him better than most. He particularly remembers a discussion they had which indicated, perhaps, that there were factors other than 1968 which probably had a bearing on his health problems in later life.

'Don was in hospital being treated for depression. After he had been in two weeks I went to see him and I said, "Do you think it really affected you the goal miss?" He said, "Yes it did, obviously. But the worst thing I ever did - that's caused the depression - was coming out of the pit."' Fox had taken early retirement from his job as a joiner at Sharlston Colliery at a time when the local coal industry was increasingly looking to shed jobs, and he was only in his fifties. Rollin remembers Fox saying to him that day, 'It's not so much about the football. I should never, ever have retired. With the goal, everybody talks about it, but over the years you get over it. People talk and I just laugh about it.'

Don's brother Neil reflects on what might have been had he been fit to play that day at Wembley. 'If it had been me kicking, I would have probably have got it, but you don't know. But I would have got over it better than Don did because I'd won so many matches with Wakefield - cup ties and important games. It would have worried me but I think I would have got over it sooner than Don. I don't think that made him depressed. But he never got over it because every year they showed the goal kick. I think that would have upset him. They didn't say he was the Lance Todd Trophy winner. It was just that he'd missed the goal.'

Son Greg Fox says of the goal miss, 'Of course, if something like that happened in your thirties, I am sure there are going to be comments made. Nobody can be part of something like that and not be affected by it at some point and I'm sure he was at the time. While I was growing up he used to tell me, "People think I'm bothered about that. I don't care. It's the others that are bothered about it. I'm not." I'm sure at the time he was. Anybody would be but it was certainly nothing to do with his depression. That came much later in life. He was 32 when he played that game and my Dad's first bouts of depression didn't come until he was in his mid-fifties. I can understand why those sort of comments are made - people's assumptions - but quite honestly, it's rubbish. It really is.'

Forty years on from the famous 'Watersplash final', on 21st August 2008, Don Fox died, aged 72, in Pinderfields Hospital, Wakefield, following a fall at the nearby Fieldhead Hospital, where he was being treated for his depression. At a subsequent inquest into Fox's death, recording a narrative verdict, the Wakefield Assistant Deputy Coroner, Mary Burke, was critical of failures in his care. Harry Waring reflected on the unhappy coincidence that two men, who together gained particular celebrity status through that much repeated clip from a rugby match also, sadly, shared something else which was to affect their lives. 'It's strange that, because Eddie died with mental illness problems as well, how two chaps who created an iconic incident in 1968, on a wet Saturday, both died with psychiatric problems.'

Joe Mullaney, summed up his thoughts about Don in a *Yorkshire Post* article at the time. 'A lot will be said and written about the player who missed that match-winning kick against Leeds at Wembley and about the death of a world class scrum-half but…' he wrote, '…I'll always remember Don Fox as the nicest, most decent man I have ever known.' At Fox's funeral at St. Luke's Church, Sharlston, on 29th August 2008, several of the surviving Trinity players from the match in 1968 were present and representatives of the Leeds club included Ken Eyre and Bill Ramsey. Don's older brother Peter referred to the game in the eulogy. A report in the *Yorkshire Post* stated that, 'He recalled after the so-called 'watersplash' final was over his brother was more concerned about his Trinity team-mates, than himself, but said this was typical. Applause broke out inside and outside the church when he declared: 'You will never meet a nicer lad."

Chapter Twenty

Reflections

Perhaps, somehow, subsequent events put into a proper context the controversies surrounding what after all was only a sporting contest. But, as I have made clear, the 1968 Rugby League Challenge Cup final was, for me, more than just a match. It was the culmination of more than a decade of growing up with, arguably, the best team in the land at the time, a fantastic journey culminating on the country's most famous sporting stage. More than anything, it was a landmark event that now, on reflection, I view as an important staging post on my journey into adulthood.

After the dreams of a sixties adolescence and the magic of Trinity's glories of that period, standing on the terraces at the end of that match was my crash-landing into the adult world, although I didn't appreciate it at the time.

The end of that match represented something else as well although, again, none of us could have known it then. I was particularly stuck by a comment made by Brian Easter, a Wakefield fan who was there that day, and a very longstanding personal friend. Easter had purchased his ticket for the Wembley final at Headingley after Trinity had won in the semi-final replay and he found himself at the Leeds end of the stadium surrounded by their jubilant supporters at the end of the game. But he consoled himself with the thought - not unreasonable at the time - that Trinity would be back next year.

He and I - and all our generation of Wakefield youngsters - had grown up with the certainty that we were likely to be back, if not next year, then the year after. We had grown up on success which we had taken for granted. But, on this occasion, we weren't going to be back next year, or the year after, or the year after that. It was to be eleven long years before the red, white and blue saw Wembley again and defeat by Widnes in 1979. So the 'Watersplash' marked not only a personal landmark in the process of some of us growing up. It undoubtedly marked the end of that glorious era of success for Trinity.

But, if there had to be an end to that era, and that wonderful decade for growing up, it could have scarcely occurred under more memorable circumstances. It certainly went out with a bang rather than a whimper and the curtain drew shut with an incredible finale that no-one present was ever likely to forget. Those who played at Wembley that day find their participation in this match always more remarked upon than any other they have taken part in during long and often distinguished careers. David Jeanes sums it up well. 'I suppose it's my claim to fame that I played in that bloody game. Not that I'd won the World Cup. Forget about that!'

It wasn't just that, for some of us, what happened that day was some sort of symbolic personal landmark or rite of passage. This final contained everything and more any sporting contest could possibly offer. That 1968 would undoubtedly live on was rightly predicted by several of those who recorded the event. Arthur Haddock, of the *Yorkshire Evening Post*, wrote shortly after the match that, 'No Rugby League game has ever been talked about so much, and looks like continuing to be discussed, as the rain-lashed Cup final… It provided something that the 90,000 paying customers and millions of televiewers will never forget.' The *Rugby Leaguer's* Tim Ashcroft summed it up well in the paper's edition published on the following Friday. 'When time has dimmed the memory of the classics at Wembley, the stark events of the 1968 trial by flood and the endurance ordeal of Leeds and Wakefield, will be imprinted in the minds of onlookers who live to see the century through.'

At the end of the reliving of this amazing drama, it is worth noting just how right these predictions were. Forty-five years on and well into the twenty-first century, the drama of Wembley 1968 has the ring of immortality. Whichever team they supported, those who were there that day and the many neutrals as well were privileged to have witnessed what is undoubtedly rugby league's most dramatic final and, probably, the most famous match in the sport's history. Phil King, in the following day's *Sunday People* took it even further, describing the final as, '…surely THE most fantastic event in British sporting history.'

That is, indeed, some claim. But few who were there that wet May day all those years ago are ever likely to forget the experience.

Acknowledgements

This book is very much a collective effort. Without the important contributions of a large number people it could never have been completed and I have received enormous help in putting it together.

I want, in particular, to thank all those I've interviewed during the course of my research into the 1968 Challenge Cup final. I am most grateful for the time they have given me and for sharing some unique memories of what remains a very special occasion.

All their names are recorded alongside their contributions but I would like to single out two; David Hebblethwaite, son of referee John Hebblethwaite and members of the Fox family - especially Don's son, Greg. Their insight was invaluable.

Others who offered significant help and advice were: Spen Allison of BARLA, Tony Capstick, Tony Collins, Tony Crosby - in particular for the loan of his 1968 scrapbook, Derek Hallas, of the Leeds Ex-Players Association, Gary

They Walked on Water

Hetherington, from Leeds Rhinos, Steve Heptinstall and the *Wakefield Express*, Richard Lewis, former Chairman of the Rugby Football League, Wakefield Trinity's Davide Longo, Joan Self of the National Meteorological Archive, Mick Slater - especially for the loan of his photographs of our 1968 Wembley trip, Geoff Wake who lent me his Wakefield Trinity Official Banquet Menu, Sarah Wickham and Amy-Jo Cameron-Williams of Huddersfield University, Gerry Wright, the Archive and Local Studies staff at Huddersfield Library, Leeds Library, Wakefield's Balne Lane Library, York Library and at the British Library, Colindale, London.

I would like to express my gratitude to Phil Caplan of Scratching Shed Publishing for his interest in and support of this project from the outset. His close connections with the Leeds club have been invaluable and his advice on my approach to the book has been most thoughtful and extremely helpful. The contributions of his colleague, Tony Hannan, have also been very much appreciated.

My family have been wonderfully supportive during the time I have been compiling this book. My wife, Julia, son, Robert, and daughter, Rebecca, have shown great patience in dealing with the problems arising from my very limited I.T. skills. In particular, Julia deserves much appreciation for the way she, more than most, has put up with my ramblings on the subject of the 1968 final for well over three decades. She might now expect a period of silence on the issue but knows full well this is highly unlikely.

I am also indebted to Mike Stephenson for his foreword and his unstinting work preserving and promoting the heritage of the sport.

It is perhaps important to make the point that attempting to record and recreate something that occurred forty-five years ago does present its difficulties. Several of the key figures involved in the match are, sadly, no longer alive. Many of those who were there that day inevitably now find it difficult to recall the exact detail.

Some of their recollections and shared experiences are contradictory so where there have been significant differences, I have felt it important to record them. In terms of the match detail, I have made use of a DVD of the BBC broadcast and included what that shows, as appropriate, in an attempt to ensure factual accuracy.

My role has been that of weaving and interpreting the various memories together in what I hope is a reasonably coherent and readable way and the responsibility for any errors is mine alone.

It has been my privilege to serve as a trustee of Try Assist - the Rugby Football League Benevolent Fund - since its formation in 2005. Knowing personally many of the former players helped by the Fund has made me very much aware of the fact that a sport that has given me and many thousands of others enormous pleasure throughout our lives does have a price to pay for a very small minority who have suffered serious injury playing.

The Fund has also had to respond to other problems facing those involved in the sport and it is very sad that mental health issues, which have in the past affected some of those featuring in this book, are only now being seriously addressed. It was an area I was particularly interested and active in during my political career.

This relaying of a truly iconic eighty minutes is dedicated to all those who Try Assist helps and supports. All royalties from the sale of this book will go to help the charity continue its vitally important work.

Bibliography

Penny Arcade, by Sammy King (Bank House Books, 2010)

An Illustrated History of Rugby League, by Robert Gate (George Weidenfield and Nicolson, 1989)

Being Eddie Waring: the Life and Times of a Sporting Icon, by Tony Hannan (Mainstream, 2008)

The Rugby League Miscellany, by David Lawrenson (Vision Sports Publishing, 2007)

Rugby League in Its Own Words, by Tim Wilkinson and Ray Gent, (Impress Sport, 2004)

The Encyclopaedia of Rugby League, by A.N. Gaulton, (Robert Hale, 1968)

The Rugby League Challenge Cup, by John Huxley, (Guinness. 1992)

100 Years of Rugby: the History of Wakefield Trinity Football Club 1873-1973, by J.C. Lindley, (Wakefield Trinity Centenary Committee, 1973)

Challenge for the Championship: The Harold Poynton Benefit Brochure, by John C. Lindley, (1968)

They Walked on Water

A People's Game: The Official History of Rugby League 1895-1995, by Geoffrey Moorhouse, (Hodder and Stoughton, 1995)

The Rugby League Miscellany, by David Lawrenson, (Vision Sports Publishing, 2007)

No Sand Dunes in Featherstone, by Robert Light (ed.), (London League Publications Ltd. 2010)

Ray French...and Rugby, by Ray French, (Scratching Shed Publishing, 2010)

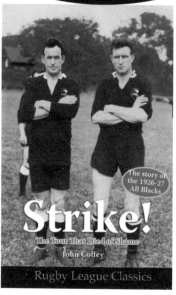

Dave Hadfield's seventh book about rugby league is devoted to one of the sport's great untold stories.

Learning Curve: The Remarkable Story of Student RL tells of how Oxford and Cambridge were conquered - places the sceptics said the game would never reach. It covers the development of 13-a-side rugby in the universities of England, Wales, Scotland and Ireland, as well as Australia, France and New Zealand. Student World Cups, Ashes series and thriving domestic comps are also featured, along with the author's inimitable and witty observations on the state of play today.

From dozens of interviews with those most closely involved, league's best-loved writer captures the spirit and dedication of the elite level, plus the humour of the lower echelons. Whether you played at university or college or not, *Learning Curve* is an unmissable treat for those who care about the future of rugby league.

Investigate our other titles and
stay up to date with all our latest releases at
www.scratchingshedpublishing.co.uk